You Can't Lose 'Em All

You Can't Lose 'Em All

The Year the Phillies Finally
Won the World Series

FRANK FITZPATRICK

Taylor Trade Publishing

Dallas, Texas

Designed by David Timmons

Published by Taylor Publishing Company
1550 West Mockingbird Lane
Dallas, Texas 75235

Library of Congress Cataloging-in-Publication Data

Fitzpatrick, Frank.
    You can't lose 'em all : the year the Phillies finally won the World
    Series / Frank Fitzpatrick. p. cm.
    Includes index.
    ISBN 0-87833-199-9 (cloth)
      1. Philadelphia Phillies (Baseball team) 2. World Series (Baseball)
    I. Title: You can't lose 'em all. II. Title.

GV875.P45 F58 2001
796.357'64'0974811—dc21   00-066645

10 9 8 7 6 5 4 3 2 1

Printed in the United States of America

In memory of Richie Ashburn, whose voice meant summer to generations of Philadelphians.

Contents

You Can't Lose 'Em All

 An Omen in a Pop-up

I dreamt the past was never past redeeming.
—RICHARD WILBUR, "THE PARDON"

Frank White's pop-up rose like a giant firefly into the glare and shadows over Veterans Stadium.

The anxious roar that had preceded Tug McGraw's delivery to the Kansas City Royals' second baseman faded as soon as the pitch, a tailing fastball, met the bat. By the time the ball reached its lofty apex, on a line above the Philadelphia Phillies' first-base dugout, 65,839 fans strained in silence.

Philadelphia will never be that quiet again.

It was 11:25 P.M. on October 21, 1980. Game 6 of the World Series was in its ninth inning. There was one out. The Phillies led the game 4–1, the Series 3–2.

"Lord," read a message on the enormous outfield scoreboard, "this is heaven!"

Phillies fans ignored the electronic optimism. They were, after all, much better acquainted with hell.

As White's pop-up lingered in the chilly nighttime air, the long, sad existence of this franchise flashed before the spectators' eyes. The Philadelphia Phillies were more than 97 years old that autumn night. Most of that long life had passed unhappily.

In their first season, 1883, the Phillies won just 17 of 98 games. Things rarely got much better.

They would lose more often than any other team in baseball history. In 1938, they won only 45 games and drew 161,111 fans—and that wasn't their worst season of the decade in either category. Every year between 1933 and 1945 they were last or next to last. Their 23-game losing streak in 1961 remained an unchallenged record. Budding stars departed as regularly as faded ones arrived. The rickety old stadium they occupied for 51 years once burned down. It also collapsed. Twice. And in 1943, a Phillies owner was banned from baseball for betting—no doubt against his woeful club.

The St. Louis Browns, who long rivaled the Phillies in futility, had moved to Baltimore a quarter-century earlier and become a smashing success. The Chicago Cubs had a second-division tradition too, but thanks largely to their ivy-covered ballpark, they at least possessed a quirky charm. And while the Boston Red Sox certainly had a cursed existence, it was one filled with the kind of memorable moments and great stars Phillies history lacked.

Only the Phillies—among the 16 franchises that comprised the major leagues for the first half of the twentieth century—had yet to win a World Series. Each of their rare good years—1915, 1950, 1976, 1977, 1978, and most memorably of all, 1964—ended with bitter disappointments.

The Philadelphia Phillies were expected to lose, just as the New York Yankees were expected to win. Their fans, in their scarred hearts, understood that. They dealt with it by booing, bellyaching to each other, cursing the night again and again. The infamous collapse of 1964—when Gene Mauch's team blew a 6½-game lead with 12 to play—had become a shared nightmare, one that permanently diminished an entire city's expectations. Optimism was impossible after that. Disaster, no matter how late in the season, how late in the game, was inevitable.

Now, craning their necks to follow White's foul, these fans wondered if that moment were at hand.

Kansas City had loaded the bases with a walk and two singles off a weary, arm-sore McGraw. There wasn't a person in the stadium, in the city, in all of baseball, who didn't believe the home team remained capable of blowing this lead, this game, this Series.

Yet what if the Phillies should somehow hold on? How would their fans react?

No frame of reference existed. Their fathers, grandfathers, and great-grandfathers had never experienced such a thing. Only two other Phillies teams had even made it to a World Series, and they had combined for just one victory—65 years earlier. True, the old Philadelphia Athletics, who moved to Kansas City in 1954 and later to Oakland, had enjoyed a few periods of sustained excellence. But Connie Mack ended them abruptly by selling off his stars, and by 1980 the A's were long forgotten. Mack's, by the way, was a typical Philadelphia response to success: If things are going well, change them.

None of the Phillies' few grand moments had occurred at home. Their first pennant, in 1915, was won in Boston; in 1950, it came in Brooklyn; this year, it was in Houston's Astrodome. Their four National League East titles came in Montreal (1976 and 1980), Chicago (1977), and Pittsburgh (1978).

So it was logical to wonder what kind of chaos might be unleashed at the southern end of Broad Street. Would celebrants dismantle the ballpark as they had Connie Mack Stadium on its final night a decade earlier? Or would they weep quietly, joyfully?

Philadelphia's baseball interest had intensified in the nine years since the Phillies moved to Veterans Stadium. As the team improved steadily, so did the size and demands of its crowds. Buoyed by Pete Rose's presence, the team drew a franchise-record 2,775,011 spectators in 1979. By 1980, a poll of National League players named Philadelphia's fans the noisiest, most supportive, and most hostile in baseball.

That September, shortstop Larry Bowa would call them the worst. In October, he called them the best. And he was right on both occasions.

The home team's players had worried about an emotional explosion all day. Those people had such an inferiority complex to shed, so much negativity to unravel, that it was easy to envision post–World Series mayhem.

"If it ends with a pop fly," thought Bowa, "they're liable to not let the thing come down."

As if to confirm those fears, a long line of mounted Philadelphia policemen had pranced their horses onto the field in the ninth inning like cavalry troops awaiting a frontier battle. There were helmeted police in the dugouts and in the seating areas. And out beyond the acres of Astroturf, in the two outfield bullpens, dozens of snarling German shepherds, tethered to yet more policemen by leather leashes, were ready to move.

"I thought," Rose said later, "that we were playing winter ball in Venezuela."

In the press level, a spacious area that wrapped around the stadium's midsection from third to first base, sportswriters were wondering how their stories and columns should read if the Phillies triumphed.

The visiting writers had not hidden their disdain for the

diffident home team. "They are the miserable millionaires," Mike Marley of the *New York Post* wrote. "Their motto is meanness, rudeness and ignorance."

Mike Lupica of the *Philadelphia Daily News*, a veteran of the Steinbrenner/Martin/Jackson chaos in the Yankees' Bronx Zoo, wrote: "The Philadelphia Phillies normally are as much fun as subway crime. . . . (They) have made the New York Yankees seem like a bunch of Fellowship of Christian Athletes."

Philadelphia's own writers had spent much of this season, and the previous one, warring with the club. "Hell's team," *Daily News* beat writer Bill Conlin still would call them ten years later. The media would make sure to temper their celebration stories with a reminder that it couldn't have happened to a grumpier group of guys.

"Be advised," wrote columnist Tom Cushman in that afternoon's *Philadelphia Daily News*, "that winning the Series will not cause the rest of the nation to forget the boorish behavior of several of the athletes involved."

"The players seem to hate the fans," said McGraw, "they seem to hate the press. And then, when they come in the clubhouse, they seem to hate each other."

Steve Carlton didn't ever speak to reporters—or to some of his teammates. Several other Phillies—including Bowa, Ron Reed, Bake McBride, Lonnie Smith, and Garry Maddox—spent sizable chunks of the season emulating their star pitcher. McBride occasionally placed a bandage over his mouth to symbolize his "No comment." The clubhouse was balkanized: Pitchers disliked hitters, veterans couldn't stand the rookies, and almost all of them were united in their distaste for blustery manager Dallas Green. After games, the Phillies frequently hid from the sportswriters in the lounge or in the training room. Writers criticized them for it, and fans, in turn, booed them for

it. Then, of course, the players despised the writers even more
for turning the fans against them.

"Philadelphia is the only city," said Mike Schmidt when the
1980 season had ended and the sting had lessened, "where you
can experience the thrill of victory and the agony of reading
about it the next day."

In a way, the Phillies' persistent losing had allowed for a
new kind of sports journalism to flower. By the early 1960s,
young Philadelphia writers like Conlin, Larry Merchant, Sandy
Grady, and Stan Hochman were perceptive enough, gifted
enough, and desperate enough to take readers behind the game.
Gone were the days of booster beat writers. These guys identified problems, pointed fingers, demanded change.

"We exposed the Phillies to the kind of daily lash formerly
wielded only by drama critics," Conlin said.

In a year or two, typewriters would vanish from pres
boxes, giving way to primitive word processors, but on this
night there were still several clacking away when catcher Bob
Boone closed in on White's pop-up.

The ball was far enough up the line that it ought to have
been the first baseman's play. Yet as the Phils catcher neared the
dugout, he couldn't locate Rose.

"C'mon, Pete," Boone thought to himself, "where are
you?"

The ball gathered speed on its descent, and Boone, a look
of near-desperation on his handsome face, reluctantly called
for it.

"Charlie Hustle, my ass," he thought.

The catcher held himself back slightly to avoid tumbling
down the steps. As, somewhat tentatively, he reached out with
his gloved right hand, Rose appeared to his left. The first baseman, a high school dropout, had decided to let the catcher, a

Stanford graduate, make the play. Sneaking a glimpse at the steps, Rose pulled up a few feet behind.

Boone, knowing he would have to act quickly to prevent Willie Mays Aikens from tagging up at third, started to turn his head an instant too soon.

Then, just as every Philadelphian feared it might, the ball bounced out of the catcher's mitt.

"His gold glove," wrote *Washington Post* columnist Thomas Boswell, "turned alchemically to lead by the black magic of Phillies history."

On this night, though, the Phillies had a Merlin of their own.

Rose's head snapped toward the ball, his hand darting in that direction like a frog's tongue toward an unsuspecting fly. The Phillies had never had a player quite like Rose, someone so cocksure of himself that he could joke about the club's horrific past and get away with it. "Philadelphia? What's that?" Rose asked agent Reuven Katz in 1979 when the possibility arose that he might become a Phillie. "Ben Franklin and last-place teams?" If this team were ever going to win, Philadelphians sensed, Rose would be the reason.

"He wanted to win so damn bad," said Reed, "that he infected everyone around him."

His arrival as a free agent in 1979 had bolstered a group of talented but insecure, eccentric, and temperamental stars, players weighed down by their own hang-ups as much as by the club's past.

"That team needed a leader," Rose said. "When I got there, they were all jealous of each other."

Mike Schmidt crippled his great natural gifts with endless introspection. Greg Luzinski and Maddox despised Green. With his constant needling and bitching, Bowa could provoke

Mother Teresa to physical assault. Reed was unusually sour. Carlton exercised by pounding his left fist into a barrel of brown rice, studied wine and Eastern religions, and didn't tolerate distractions. And most of them practiced a studied cool, a strutting "nothing-can-bother-me" attitude that drove the wildly emotional Green crazy.

"That 'macho cool' crap," the manager called it.

Three years in a row, 1976–78, outstanding Phillies teams had won the NL East easily, only to justify their fans' pessimism by self-destructing in the play-offs. Rose was supposed to be the antidote. Hell, he didn't care about being cool. Just the way he looked belied coolness—a salad-bowl haircut, garish clothes, a perpetual sneer. He didn't strut, he sprinted. And there was nothing studied about him at all. One ex-teammate in Cincinnati remarked that nothing in the world traveled quite so fast as a thought moving from Rose's mind to his lips.

In time, he helped convince the Phillies they really were good enough to win it all. He stood apart from them, as if he were a hired consultant, and advised them on the path to baseball fulfillment. He told them why they had failed in the past. He preached focus and was the first player in the clubhouse every day. Maybe most importantly, he told Schmidt how much opposing pitchers feared him, and the third baseman responded with the best seasons of his career.

"When I got there, Mike felt like he was the best player in the league maybe three or four days a week," said Rose. "Afterward, he knew he was the best seven days."

And when many of them declared war on the local press, Rose continued as their garrulous, ungrammatical spokesman.

Now, as the dropped ball neared the turf, Rose extended his right hand behind him for balance. Palms out, bowed forward at the waist as if he were a tap dancer performing an act-ending flourish, he snatched the ball almost before Boone knew he had dropped it. Flicking his glove back powerfully toward his body, he turned menacingly toward the base runners, bounced the ball once on the turf for punctuation, and returned it, with a pointed underhanded flip, to McGraw.

The crowd, many of whom would be among the 1½ million lining Broad Street for the next day's victory parade, took an instant to comprehend what they had just seen. The deafening bellow that followed shook the stadium. People wept, laughed, and hugged whomever happened to be next to them. Several of the police horses reared back nervously, startled by the burst of noise. The dogs, one of which had snapped at McGraw's glove when the reliever stood to warm up an inning earlier, barked and strained at the ends of their leashes.

The symbolism was too perfect. Rose had slapped down bad fortune with a quick jab from his gloved hand. One out remained, but the game and the legacy of failure were over. The Phillies were going to win their first world championship.

"We couldn't lose now if fucking Babe Ruth came up," Bowa thought to himself as Willie Wilson came to the plate. "Now how the hell am I going to get back to the dugout?"

◆ ◆ ◆

It might have been one of the most spiritual moments in sports history. Rose's catch—and the Phillies championship that followed minutes later—was faith fulfilled, the unthinkable realized. An entire city had been redeemed.

No baseball fans anywhere had waited longer. None had more reason to celebrate. Fervent followers of other teams merely prayed for a championship but in Philadelphia, they prayed for the miracle they knew would be necessary *before* the gods at last allowed them relief.

With Rose, like John the Baptist preparing the way, salvation had come at last.

There are Philadelphians who swear the noise didn't stop for 24 hours. From the moment McGraw followed Rose's catch by striking out Wilson until work crews swept Broad Street clear of the victory parade's litter the following night, the old city quivered with a raucous excitement.

That night in South Philadelphia, they did the Mummer's strut. In Kensington, they swung from the Market Street El's lofty girders. In North Philadelphia, celebrants skipped along the roofs of parked cars as they made their way down Broad Street. Any World Series victory provokes an outburst of joy and civic pride, but it's hard to imagine anyone ever savored a championship more than Philadelphia's baseball fans in 1980.

Brooklyn exploded in 1955, but the Dodgers were perennial contenders and the wait was nowhere near the Phillies' 97 years. What would it have meant to Kansas City had the Royals won? That a 12-year wait was over? What if the Yankees had triumphed? Whoopee! What's that, No. 23?

The Philadelphia Flyers' 1974 Stanley Cup, which also touched off a great downtown celebration, couldn't compare. That National Hockey League franchise had been just seven years old, and the majority of Philadelphians, not raised with hockey, still thought icing belonged on a cake.

But every row house in the city held a story about suffering with the Phillies, about the unused 1964 World Series tickets kept in a cigar box, about the losing streak in 1961, about the way people snickered when they revealed their baseball allegiance.

"My dad lived and died with the Phillies, literally. He was listening to a game when he had a heart attack," said Jim Galloway, a Philadelphian who moved to southern California in the early 1970s. "I loved them, too. When I came out here, I'd go to Dodgers games with a Phillies hat on. These fans usually don't say much to anyone, but people would laugh at me. I was in line at a concession stand one time, and this guy walks past and shouts, '1964!'

"I thought about him, and about my dad, the night they finally won the Series."

These fans now cheered themselves as much as the Phillies. They had heard the Philadelphia jokes for so long that, perhaps to protect themselves from the sting, they had joined in, developing a negative attitude about their hometown that shocked outsiders. Everyone knew W. C. Fields's epitaph ("On the whole, I'd rather be in Philadelphia.") mocked the city. But people forgot that Fields *was* a Philadelphian. You can't make fun of my city, the thinking went, because I'm going to beat you to it.

"I know how the city feels," McGraw said. "It's like a man shows up out of nowhere and he tells you, 'Here, I've got a magic carpet, and I'm going to give you a ride on it. C'mon, get on, and we'll soar away.'

"And the people get on and right away that man yanks that carpet right out from under them. And this keeps happening, and pretty soon the people are afraid to believe, they're afraid to get on that magic carpet ride."

Once the nation's capital, the continent's first great city, America's manufacturing center, Philadelphia, since the 1950s, had become an increasingly insignificant point between Washington and New York. The fact that its baseball team, in the words of one fan at Veterans Stadium the night they finally won, "either sucked or choked" didn't help.

"I don't think the Phillies have ever known what the voice of the crowd was saying," wrote *Philadelphia Daily News* columnist Larry McMullen, "not when it cheered, not when it wailed and moaned. In all of the team's history, its players, these outsiders, haven't been the sufferers. . . . All they've ever been is carriers."

That first taste of victory never was sweeter.

Someday the Cubs or the Red Sox will win another championship, touching the hearts of their much-pained fans. But there will be someone to remind them that, even though it was many years ago, this had happened before.

On the night of October 21, 1980, dancing Phillies fans recognized that nothing matched the first time. Who, after all, talks of their second sexual encounter?

◆ ◆ ◆

As happens with any championship team after a few decades, a kind of gauzy mythology begins to shroud the reality.

The 1980 Phillies, according to their legend, were a group of talented, underachieving individuals herded together by Green's constant prodding. The manager, and on at least one occasion, the general manager, bitched and bellowed—in public and behind closed clubhouse doors—until the Phillies finally united in September, finally bought into Green's "We Not I" philosophy that had made them snicker in spring training.

Green's obscenity-laden August tirade in Pittsburgh and general manager Paul Owens's locker-room challenge in San Francisco a few weeks later get much of the credit for the Phillies late-season surge. It was said that those tongue-lashings forced the players to reexamine themselves and, Voila!, the season was saved.

But something much more complex drove the 1980 Phillies to a world championship. It combined ample doses of anger, fate, and talent, but there was still something else. Questions about just what it was remain unresolved.

It could have been either Green or the players themselves who rallied the team. If the manager's outburst really pulled them together, then why did the players decide they needed to meet in Chicago the following day? Reed insists that the August 11 session in Wrigley Field's cramped visitors locker room was no confirmation of Green's lecture. Some Phillies, he said, actually derided it.

"We said, 'The hell with Dallas, the hell with the coaching staff,'" recalled Reed. "'Let's win it for ourselves.'"

Was it "We Not I" that finally kicked in? Or "Us vs. Them"?

Their play-off failures and clubhouse chaos, as well as their battles with fans and the media, had built up quite a storehouse of ill will. Then, in August, when a repeat of the Phillies' 1979 flop seemed likely, all the naysayers in the stands and in the press box revived.

"There was this undercurrent of suspicion surrounding our team," McGraw said. "We were labeled spoiled, overpaid underachievers. We didn't have the guts and so forth. So whenever we'd win a big game, you'd hear guys say, 'Take that overpaid crap and stick it up your ass.'"

And how can the chaotic events of September 29 be explained?

On that Monday night at Veterans Stadium, the start of the season's final week, the Phillies were at their dysfunctional worst, still much closer to team turmoil than team togetherness.

Green benched three regulars and, after his team rallied for a 6–5 win in 15 innings, suggested he had players who didn't want the Phillies to win. Bowa ripped the manager on his pregame radio show. Later that night, the shortstop obscenely maligned the fans. Maddox angrily confronted a writer, and a night later he removed himself from the lineup.

Why, when Green ran out during the introductions before

Game 1 of the National League Championship Series, did Phillies players react as if Josef Mengele had come to join them?

Watching it on film remains difficult. Bowa and Maddox turn away from the manager, and Boone extends a hand with all the enthusiasm of a root-canal patient opening wide.

If they were so tightly knit in September, why were so many continuing to act in their own self-interests midway through the NLCS?

For example, after splitting the first two play-off games at home, Green told his players that wives would not be permitted to accompany them to Houston. That was a break with postseason traditions, but the manager believed the Phils' recent play-off flops demanded such changes.

The edict wasn't easy for the wives to accept—and, consequently, wasn't easy for the players to swallow. Baseball spouses like to think of themselves as essential appendages of the players. Talk to them about their husbands and you'll hear them, in all sincerity, say things like, "We were traded to L.A. that year." The wives had attended most home games, as well as many on the road, and were as caught up as anyone in the Phillies' end-of-season drama.

So, with their husbands' approval, Donna Schmidt, Sheena Bowa, Jean Luzinski, Sue Boone, and others went anyway.

Finally, how can the scene in the Phillies post–World Series locker room be explained?

The club's first world championship was only an hour old. Champagne still dripped from Green's thickly curled hair. You might have expected the vociferous manager, fueled by beer, champagne, and adrenaline, to prattle on endlessly about how his team had overcome its history.

In similar situations, once the formal interviews are done, managers tend to reflect on pivotal moments from the long season and enumerate the contributions of each player. They'll gaze misty-eyed into the distant past and speak hopefully of the future. But when Green was asked about his plans for 1981, it was rather jarring to hear his response.

"I don't want to put up with another year like this one," he said.

That wasn't just irony. He meant it.

And at that very moment, Carlton, the winning pitcher in Game 6, sat alone in the trainer's room. He ought to have been slapping and hugging his teammates, gasping for air beneath a Niagara Falls of champagne. After all, when Carlton came to Philadelphia in 1972, his first Phillies team won only 32 games without him. He had been their rock. What player could possibly appreciate this championship more?

Instead, Carlton sipped champagne by himself. Not the Great Western brand his teammates drank either. That apparently wasn't good enough for his delicate palate. He clutched a magnum of the good stuff.

At one point, rookie reliever Dickie Noles entered the room, hugged Carlton and started to spray him with champagne. The great pitcher held up a big hand and shook his head negatively. Noles pulled back the bottle and retreated.

Take away the significant elements of its history and its fans, and the story of the 1980 Phillies is, until the last possible moment, not a warm one. It will never translate into one of those sappy TV sports movies. Its heroes were too conflicted. Its themes too discordant.

"This," recalled Jayson Stark, who covered the team for the *Philadelphia Inquirer*, "was not the Good Ship Phillies."

◆ ◆ ◆

If any single event unified the 1980 Phillies, allowed them to transcend their petty feuds, crystallized for them everything that had been going on outside their Veterans Stadium bunker, it was the march down Broad Street the morning after the World Series ended.

As they stood atop those flatbed trailers, rolling slowly through the smiling masses, the Phillies underwent some sort of spiritual awakening. Broad Street had become their road to Damascus. At that moment, for a first time, they understood that it didn't matter why they won, or how. Only that they did.

It was then that they realized the suffering their fans had experienced in the last century, the happiness they felt now.

"I don't think I could ever see a more awesome sight in sports," said Rose on the victory march from Center City to JFK Stadium. "Just seeing the same expression on a million faces."

Fans tossed flowers. "And not those plastic flowers," said Owens, "real fresh flowers. Roses." The petals stuck to the GM's face, held there by tears.

"I had imagined the parade would be relaxing," said Boone. "Instead it was this monstrous emotional high, probably the greatest moment of my life."

Ten years later, when the 1980 Phillies gathered for their first reunion, players and team officials wondered how the passing decade might have altered the team's psyche.

Would Schmidt still be as emotionally distant? Green so belligerent? Bowa so annoyingly hyperactive? And what would they talk about? Game 5 of the NLCS? Game 6 of the Series?

"You know, there was only one thing that every one of those guys brought up," said Owens of that 1990 event. "The parade. Everyone mentioned how much it had affected them."

Well, maybe not everyone.

As the Phillies moved down sunny Broad Street that October day, Ron Reed was sitting alone in Philadelphia International Airport, waiting for a plane to take him home.

Even if you were a Philadelphian who never set foot in the Phillies clubhouse, never read one of the city's four daily newspapers, and didn't go to the parade, that 1980 season—especially its last 3½ weeks—had to take your breath away.

"No one," said Boone, "who lived through it will ever forget."

All the moments that made it unforgettable rest there now in the city's collective memory like signposts to the promised land. Mention 1980 to a Philadelphian and it still triggers a chill.

The three-run comeback in the bottom of the 15th inning to beat the Cubs on September 29. Schmidt's long game-winning homer in the opener of the final series at Montreal. His longer one in the tenth inning a day later to give the Phillies the NL East title.

The near-ceaseless thrills of their unmatched NLCS with Houston: The disputed triple play. A runaway Rose decking Bruce Bochy. Manny Trillo's relay throws. The stunning eighth-inning rally against rally-proof Nolan Ryan. Maddox's winning hit and last-out catch in Game 5.

Then the welcome relief of the World Series: McBride's Game 1 home run. Dickie Noles knocking George Brett on his hemorrhoids in Game 4. The historic Boone–Rose hookup in Game 6. McGraw's strikeout of Willie Wilson. Schmidt's uncharacteristic leap into the reliever's arms.

All that and much more was crammed into just 23 days. Now, as Philadelphians wait without much hope for a second championship, that brief shining moment seems like it lasted an eternity.

At its delicious conclusion, no one wanted the 1980 season to end. So it's hard to recall that eight months earlier, in Clearwater, no one was certain it would begin.

Once the threatening labor problems were set aside and, on a cool Friday evening in South Philadelphia, the Phillies season started, the excitement didn't build gradually. Only the frustrations did.

The Phillies, except for Carlton, ran hot and cold for more than four months. Their lack of consistency was no surprise. They endured a midseason drug scandal when they nearly overdosed on bitterness. Rose's highly publicized divorce didn't help. There were injuries. And, punctuating everything, like windswept whitecaps on an already roiled sea, was the constant newsprint war between Green and his players.

"Every day," said Schmidt, "you would walk into the clubhouse and wonder what was waiting for you today. Who said who was a gutless jerk? Who said who was lazy? Or who was selfish? It was a soap opera, a yearlong soap opera. But man, did it have a glorious end."

Nineteen eighty began, as all seasons do, with questions. Was 1979 an aberration? Or the beginning of the end of the most interesting and successful period in the ballclub's history? Would the Phillies survive a full season of Green? Would Green survive a full season of the Phillies? Was Luzinski done? Would the physically fragile rotation stay healthy?

But the one question that loomed largest when the Phillies reported to training camp that spring concerned baseball's labor situation.

As the Players Association became more emboldened, the owners more stubborn, and the economic issues more muddled, baseball's labor strife appeared nearly intractable that spring. The sport had endured a strike in 1972 and a lockout in 1976. The landmark Andy Messersmith case, which established free agency after a century of the reserve clause's sanctioned slavery, was just four years old in 1980.

Salaries skyrocketed and the owners, suddenly under siege, searched for a way to emasculate the revolutionary free-agency system.

The dispute dominated spring training. The Phillies may have been affected more than most teams. Boone, as the National League's player representative, was a major figure in the negotiations. The talk distracted him.

"There was a question-and-answer session every day, and I really think it took away from my preparations at training camp," said Boone, who never found his offense that year.

Finally, on April 1, with no compromise in sight, the players voted to end spring training. They would start the regular season on time, but they set a strike deadline of May 22.

The Phillies, for once, hung together. They worked out for the last week-and-a-half under Green. But pessimistic Philadelphians knew what to expect next in the macabre script guiding this team's destiny: The Phils would race out to an enormous early season lead. Then, just as they became uncatchable and their fans felt safe to rejoice, a strike would end the season.

Fortunately, an agreement came at the eleventh hour on May 22. It was a weak and incomplete settlement, one directly responsible for the strike that came the following season, but 1980 was no longer threatened.

Still the Phillies stuttered and muttered. Until, when it was very nearly too late, they saved their season, saved their fans' sanity, saved themselves from themselves.

"I think the 1980 season was a matter of timing," said Carlton, years later, when he was talking again and a lot of people began to wish he'd stop. "Everything came together at the end."

Chapter 1

A Long, Lamentable Legacy of Losing

Since 1915 I have been cheering for the Philadelphia Phillies, and if that doesn't take character, what does? In such circumstances it is traditional to say, 'I supported them in good years and bad.' There were no good years. I cheered in bad and worse.

JAMES MICHENER, *NEW YORK TIMES*, 1978

Philadelphia, being the birthplace of America and the Constitution, liked to fancy itself the City of Firsts. And once the Phillies arrived, locals pointed out, many lasts.

Examining the franchise's history is akin to reading the Book of Job. The calamities are endless. The degradation unspeakable. It's easy to see why generations of Philadelphians never followed the examples of Chicago or Boston baseball fans in believing that their team was cursed.

Cursed would have been an improvement. This franchise was doomed.

Banned owners. Broke owners. Phantom owners. A racist manager. A manager who quit one game into a season. A manager whose team quit 150 games into a season. A great pitcher who died of typhoid. A great hitter who tumbled into Niagara

Falls. The worst collapse in baseball history—in both the pennant race *and* stadium divisions.

So dismal is the Phillies story that it actually helped change baseball forever. If Curt Flood had been traded anywhere else in 1969, the economic earthquake his challenge of the reserve clause touched off might have been delayed for years.

"Philadelphia has as long a baseball tradition as any city in America," said Phillies outfielder Harry Anderson in the 1950s. "But for a long time now, it's been a baseball graveyard."

Let's say you were a Philadelphian born in the first decade of the twentieth century. You loved baseball, preferred the National League, and by 1917 had become a Phillies fan. Well, by 1948, assuming you hadn't been hospitalized or switched allegiances, you would still be waiting. Waiting not just for a World Series, not just for a pennant, not even for a near miss. Thirty-one years after you gave your heart to the Phillies, you would not yet have experienced a single winning season!

Through American participation in two world wars, through the Great Depression, through the integration of the game, through the home-run revolution and Babe Ruth, the Philadelphia Phillies never once finished over .500. In those three-plus decades, they could manage as many as 70 wins just twice, averaging nearly 95 losses a year in an era of 154-game seasons.

"You can't imagine how it was," said longtime Philadelphia sportswriter Mayer Brandschain. "Most people just gave up on the Phillies. If they liked baseball, they followed the Athletics. There was no point in cheering for the Phillies, because you knew that at the end of the season things would be the same. They would be in seventh or eighth place. Sixth in a good year."

Consider 1930, simultaneously one of their most memorable and embarrassing seasons. That year's team, with Chuck

Klein and Lefty O'Doul, set dozens of club records that still stand. Its team batting average was .315. O'Doul batted .383. Klein hit .386 with 40 home runs and a mind-boggling 170 RBIs. He and O'Doul combined to score 280 runs. Those two plus Pinky Whitney each topped the 200-hit mark.

And where did that Phillies juggernaut finish?

Last.

Fifty games under .500.

Forty games behind the first-place Cardinals.

◆ ◆ ◆

It should come as no surprise that the Phillies were left on Philadelphia's doorstep.

In 1883, the National League team in Worcester, Massachusetts, folded. The young league, concerned about competition from the new American Association, decided it had to get back into the Philadelphia market.

The city had a baseball tradition going back to 1833 and had been a charter member of the NL in 1876. But the National League expelled the Athletics at the end of that first year when they couldn't come up with enough cash to fund an end-of-season road trip.

The old Athletics' fiscal fate was an appropriate omen. If there is a theme that runs through the story of the Phillies in the twentieth century, it is—more than a lack of talent—a lack of money. With the 38-year exception of the Carpenter family and their DuPont fortune, the Phillies were run by underfunded, unstable ownership. Between 1903 and 1943, they had ten different owners and won only a single pennant.

The first owner was Al Reach, a one-time Athletics star who had started the sporting goods company that bore his name. He and Philadelphia lawyer John Rogers purchased the bankrupt Worcester Brown Stockings and moved them to Philadelphia. All they really bought was the name. The team's players had all gone elsewhere. Reach called them the Phillies, and that is his legacy.

"It tells you who we are and where we're from," explained Reach.

One hundred seventeen years later, the Philadelphia Phillies remain the oldest one-name, one-city franchise in baseball. Through the years, unsuccessful efforts were made to call them the Live Wires and the Blue Jays. Their fans have called them much worse. Reach's original nickname, uninspiring as it may have been, proved to be a winner even if his teams did not.

Misfortune quickly found the Phillies and never really left. Their first great player, pitcher Charles Ferguson, won 99 games between 1884 and 1887. In 1888, at 25, he was dead of typhoid fever.

Their next star, hard-drinking outfielder Ed Delahanty, was found dead beneath Niagara Falls in 1903. He was Washington's property by then, but his tragic death seemed to typify the Phillies' fate.

The team initially played at Recreation Park, at 24th Street and Columbia Avenue in North Philadelphia. But in 1887, the Phillies opened a new $100,000 ballpark, on a slight rise along Broad Street, between Huntingdon and Lehigh avenues. It stood just seven blocks from where the American League's Athletics would build Shibe Park in 1909.

The Philadelphia Ballpark, which later was renamed Baker Bowl after the man who owned the Phillies from 1913 to 1930, was a state-of-the-art facility when it opened. Its wooden infrastructure was braced with steel and sheathed in eye-appealing brick at its main entrance. Architecturally handsome with its twin turrets, the park contained several revolutionary features, including stalls for 55 horse-drawn carriages beneath its grand-stands.

Twenty thousand people toured the ballpark on the day it was completed. Philadelphians were extremely proud. Sports-writers called it the showplace of baseball.

And, in 1894, it burned to the ground.

No one is certain how the fire started. Arson or a plumber's torch were suspected. Surveying the wreckage, Reach noted that all that remained were the main entrance and a portion of the centerfield wall. He and Rogers ordered it rebuilt. Seating capacity was increased from 12,000 to 18,800. This time there was more steel and less wood. But the upkeep proved a burden to a series of penny-pinching owners, and the stadium soon gained a reputation as a flimsy firetrap. The few spectators who attended games there called it "The Dump on the Hump" or worse. Although Baker Bowl was a stately pleasure dome when Al Reach built it for his Phillies in 1887, by the 1930s it "bore a striking resemblance to a rundown men's room," wrote sports-writer Red Smith.

On August 6, 1903, during a Phillies–Cardinals game, the screams of two young women on the street below caused many fans to crowd onto a leftfield balcony. The excess weight over-burdened the supports, and the balcony collapsed. Twelve spec-tators were killed, and 200 injured. Dozens of lawsuits were filed against the financially strapped organization.

To prove that they were able to muster bad fortune no matter where they played, the Phillies moved to the Athletics' Columbia Park while repairs were being made. Four days later, one of the longest stretches of sustained rain in Philadelphia history began. Nine consecutive home games were post-poned—another of the dubious records the Phillies still held at the start of the second millennium.

While thrills were infrequent in those years, spills were

not. In 1898, Cincinnati catcher Tommy Corcoran tripped as he rounded third base. Sprawled in the dirt, Corcoran discovered a wire beneath the dirt. Following it, umpires were led to the home team's centerfield clubhouse. There they discovered that backup catcher Morgan Murphy had been gazing through a tiny hole with a pair of binoculars, stealing signals.

The wire was a telegraph line that extended back into the Phillies dugout. Murphy had been stealing pitches. He tapped once for a fastball, twice for a curve, and three times for a change-up. Rogers explained to chagrined league officials that he knew what had been taking place but hadn't realized the practice was illegal. It was a measure of the team's abilities that even with the stolen signs they finished sixth.

From 1891 to 1895, Delahanty, Sam Thompson, and Billy Hamilton made up a Phillies outfield that might have been baseball's best. In 1899, Delahanty hit .410, Nap Lajoie hit .378, and the Phils won 94 games, a total that would stand as a club record until 1976.

When the American League debuted in 1901, Reach's partner in the sporting goods company, Ben Shibe, was granted a franchise. Shibe was the firm's money man, and Reach and Rogers couldn't compete with him for players. The Philadelphia Athletics stole Lajoie and three Phillies pitchers in their first season. The Phillies got an injunction that prevented the defectors from playing in Philadelphia, but they signed with other AL teams.

The A's, immediately successful on the field, and with colorful characters like eccentric pitcher Rube Waddell, dominated the city's sporting scene in the century's early years. Phillies attendance fell to abysmal levels. In 1902, the Phillies drew 112,066 fans, their all-time twentieth-century low. That same year, Delahanty jumped to Washington in the AL.

By 1903, Reach and Rogers had more good sense than

cash. They unloaded the team not long before its stadium fell down. The new owner, Philadelphia stockbroker James Potter, burdened by the disaster's lawsuits and attendance that remained under 200,000, did the same in 1904, turning over the team to minority owner Bill Shettsline. The front-office merry-go-round continued. A syndicate of local politicians purchased the club before the 1909 season and sold it later that same year to Horace Fogel.

Fogel's stewardship would not prove to be a glorious chapter in team history—as anyone who took the time to check into his background could have predicted.

First, he had once managed the New York Giants, a brief endeavor made memorable only by his efforts to convert Christy Mathewson, one of the sport's legendary pitchers, into a first baseman. Second, Fogel had since become a Philadelphia sportswriter, generally not among the wealthy class of optimists from whom owners traditionally emerge.

Fogel immediately failed in an effort to change the team's name to the Live Wires, an incongruous choice that would have been like calling the equally bad St. Louis Browns the St. Louis Hot Pinks.

But as it turned out, Fogel was a shrewd investor. He hadn't put any of his money into the Phillies. He was, in fact, a front man for Charles Taft, the brother of the rotund U.S. president, because the league frowned on dual ownership and Taft already operated the Chicago Cubs.

Fogel hung on until the league forced him out after the 1912 season. Seems he had been telling his old sportswriter buddies that the 1912 season was fixed. He might have been right, since the era's gamblers operated brazenly at Baker Bowl and most other big-league stadiums. That condition wouldn't change until the aftermath of the Black Sox scandal in 1919.

Earlier in 1919, by the way, the last-place Phillies arrived in Chicago for an August series accompanied by rumors that the Cubs pitcher was going to throw the first game. Chicago manager Fred Mitchell reacted by pulling that day's starter and replacing him with Grover Cleveland Alexander. But the Phillies, who finished 47½ games out of first, won anyway, 3–0. Phils manager Gavvy Cravath was asked his reaction to the sordid speculation. "I don't know why they've got to bring a thing like this up just because we win one," he said. "We're liable to win a game anytime."

Fogel's ouster led to a sale to another syndicate, headed by Pittsburgh Pirates' secretary William Locke. Locke, perhaps choosing the lesser of two evils, died six months into his tenure. His partner, William Baker, took over.

Suddenly, a glimmer of light appeared on Broad Street. The Phillies had been able to sign pitcher Grover Cleveland Alexander in 1911 for a bargain price in part because some other clubs were concerned about the pleasant Nebraska farmboy's drinking.

The right-hander won 22 games in 1913. Tom Seaton added 27. And in Fred Luderus, the Phillies finally had found a left-handed hitter capable of taking advantage of Baker Bowl's ridiculously short rightfield fence, just 280 feet down the line.

"Baker Bowl had the charm of a city dump, but not the size," wrote Red Smith of its unusual dimensions. "If the right-fielder had beer on his breath, as he frequently did, the first baseman could smell it."

First baseman Luderus hit 18 homers. Cravath, though right-handed, led the major leagues with 19. Their combined 37 surpassed the total of all but two major-league teams, and the Phillies finished second, 12½ games behind John McGraw's Giants. The attendance of 470,000 set a franchise record.

With a rapidly improving team and a growing fan base, the Phillies were due for some bad news. It arrived in 1914 with the formation of the rival Federal League. The underfunded Phillies immediately lost several players, including Seaton and short-stop Mickey Doolan, and fell back to a more familiar sixth place in 1914.

New manager Pat Moran rebuilt the pitching staff in 1915. Led by Alexander's 31 wins, 1.22 ERA, 36 complete games, 12 shutouts, and 376 innings, Philadelphia's staff ERA was a league-best 2.15. Cravath was now the king of the home run, hitting a career-best 24. That led the league, as did his totals in RBIs, runs, walks, and total bases. Luderus hit .315.

With the rest of the league now weakened by the second— and last—Federal League season, Moran's Phillies won the fran-chise's first pennant with a record of 90–62, seven games better than the second-place Boston Braves.

In the World Series opener at Baker Bowl, Alexander beat the Red Sox's Ernie Shore 3–1. There is a photo that shows the aftermath of Game 1. Thousands of Philadelphia men, in coats and ties, wander aimlessly around the field. The most common expression on their faces does not seem to be joy or excitement. It is bewilderment, as if they are simultaneously pondering two questions: "Did we really just see the Phillies win a World Series game?" and "Will we ever see it again?"

The answers were "Yes" and "If you live another 65 years."

The Phillies lost the next four games to the Red Sox. Boston's second-year pitcher Babe Ruth grounded out in his only Series at bat, but never set foot on the mound. The Red Sox needed just three pitchers—Shore, Dutch Leonard, and Rube Foster—to beat the Phils.

Moran did nothing to enhance his reputation as a manage-rial genius in the series. In Game 5, won by the Red Sox 5–4, the Phillies manager had his best hitter, Cravath, try a 3–2 suicide squeeze with the bases loaded and nobody out. He bunted into a double play. The Phillies didn't score and lost by a run.

Baker didn't help much either. The owner had installed extra bleachers in front of the grandstands in leftfield and centerfield to take advantage of the demand for World Series tickets. In Game 5, Boston's Harry Hooper, who had hit just three homers all year, drove two into those appealingly close seats as the Red Sox eliminated the Phillies.

Whatever new fans the World Series created soon faded away. And no mechanism, save boosterish sportswriters, existed to try to lure them back. Marketing and public relations would remain unknown concepts in baseball for several more decades. In 1923, for example, the Phillies had a young fan taken to jail when he refused to return a foul ball. The kid had a wealthy father who fought the club and won. The squabble made foul balls fair game everywhere, marking perhaps the only time the Phillies could claim responsibility for creating a cherished baseball tradition.

In 1916, Philadelphia actually won one more game than in the previous year, but finished second to Brooklyn by 2½ games. That team drew a record 515,365 fans, a franchise mark that would stand until the postwar season of 1946. The following year they won 87 and were runners-up again.

That's when the great darkness fell.

◆ ◆ ◆

Instead of cherishing Alexander, Baker worried only that he might lose the wonderfully gifted but personally flawed pitcher. When the U.S. entered World War I in 1917, the Phillies owner's anxiety intensified. Knowing his star was eligible to be drafted, Baker fretted that Alexander would be killed or injured. So on November 11, 1917, he impulsively traded the great pitcher for $60,000 and two players who never amounted to anything

(Mike Prendergast and Pickles Dillhoefer). Alexander did go to war. He also returned and won another 183 games.

The Phillies never could seem to recapture the spirit of 1915, but in 1927 they did see a repeat of the 1903 stadium disaster. On May 14, as spectators huddled beneath a rightfield roof in a rainstorm, a section of the grandstands collapsed. This time only one fan died, but 50 were hurt. Watching the Phillies wasn't only fruitless, it was dangerous. The team temporarily moved up Lehigh Avenue to the A's Shibe Park, a handsome steel and concrete stadium that would become their permanent home a decade later.

With Klein, O'Doul, and Don Hurst, the Phils were a remarkable offensive club in the late 1920s and early 1930s. But they committed 236 errors, and the pitching was so horrible they could never contend. No team has ever come close to matching the 6.71 ERA they compiled in 1930.

They also were practically forgotten in their hometown as Philadelphia's attention was riveted on Mack's A's. The Athletics won three consecutive pennants in 1929, 1930, and 1931, and with Jimmie Foxx, Lefty Grove, Mickey Cochrane, and Al Simmons, they were among the best ballclubs ever.

During those forgettable 1930s, the great wall that ran from centerfield to rightfield at Baker Bowl was covered by a soap ad that read, "The Phillies use Lifebuoy." Some disgruntled fan painted an addendum that accurately reflected the city's feelings toward its NL representative: "And they still stink."

In retrospect, it's remarkable that it was the Phillies, and not the A's, who survived in Philadelphia. The Athletics, for all their horrible seasons and Mack's maddening habit of selling future Hall of Famers, won five World Series. The Athletics' all-time roster was filled with big names, and they almost always outdrew their pathetic NL rivals.

It was simply their bad luck that in the early 1950s, when

established but struggling franchises at last began to relocate, the Phillies had much more stable ownership and were just a few years removed from a pennant-winning season.

"A few years before," said Brandschain, "and it would have been the Phillies who left and the A's who stayed."

Baker died in 1930, but not before he traded O'Doul. The owner and his wife left much of their stock to a team secretary, Mary Nugent. Her husband, Gerald, took over the club. His training? He was a shoe salesman.

Nugent kept the team for a decade, during which his principal occupation seemed to be seeing how quickly he could unload talent. Proving that he knew more about brogans than baseball, he traded Whitney and Hurst. Then, on November 21, 1933, he sent Klein, a Triple Crown winner and future Hall of Famer, to the Cubs for three nobodies and $65,000. Nugent later would trade Dick Bartell, Bucky Walters, and Dolph Camilli, all competent ballplayers.

The lousy attendance got worse. Between 1933 and 1938, the Phillies never drew 250,000 fans in a season. During one Phillies–Cubs game, bored sportswriters began dumping cups of water from their lofty press-box perch. Seeing their antics, Nugent yelled in their direction, "Gentlemen, we have patrons downstairs!" That prompted Chicago sportswriter Warren Brown to reply: "My God, there's a story!"

Finally, midway through the 1938 season, the Phillies abandoned Baker Bowl for cotenancy with the A's at Shibe Park. For many Philadelphians and national sportswriters, there was something sacrilegious about the new team in a ballpark the A's had, for the most part, bathed in glory.

"There, where the ghosts of [Chief] Bender and [Eddie] Plank and [Frank] Baker and [Zip] Collins and Cochrane still cavort in their brilliance," wrote columnist Bob Considine, "where every retrospect is pleasing, there you see the Phillies."

Doc Prothro managed the Phillies from 1939 to 1941. His teams finished last each year and averaged 107 losses a season. In one of those seasons, a frustrated young pitcher approached Prothro.

"After pitching on this club for a couple of months, I'm not sure whether I'm in the big leagues or not," he whined.

"Son," said Prothro, "don't ever think you're not in the big leagues. We may not be a big-league club, but we are playing against big-league clubs."

In 1939, after the Phillies ended an eight-game losing streak by beating the Giants, several of them were arrested for throwing bottles out of their New York hotel-room windows. Learning their identities, a police sergeant ordered his younger colleagues to release the Phillies.

"Let them have their fun," he said. "They don't get much chance to celebrate."

With both Philadelphia teams sharing Shibe Park, there soon was little difference between them. The Athletics and Phillies each finished last in their first season together, 1938, and again in 1940, 1941, 1942, and 1945. By 1943, Nugent didn't have two penny-loafers to scrape together.

Word spread that the Phillies were on the market again, news which must have energized shoe salesmen and sportswriters everywhere. One of those interested was Bill Veeck, the son of a former Chicago Cubs president and then the owner of a minor-league club. Veeck contacted Nugent and told him he had a plan.

He had seen the great Negro League players. He knew Satchel Paige, Roy Campanella, Luke Easter, and dozens of others would be stars in the big leagues if they were allowed to play. He also knew there was no way baseball's owners were ready to integrate by conventional means.

What Veeck proposed to Nugent was simple and far too revolutionary for staid baseball in 1943. Sell your practically worthless club, Veeck said, and I'll fill the Phillies roster with the Negro League stars. That way everyone would be happy. The Phillies would not only be saved but successful. The other owners wouldn't have to worry about integration. And a whole new market—African-American fans—would be opened for baseball.

"(Nugent) expressed a willingness to accept it," Veeck later recalled. "I had not the slightest doubt that in 1944, a war year, the Phillies would have leaped from seventh place to the pennant."

Shrewd as he was, Veeck made one miscalculation. He felt the need to inform baseball commissioner Judge Kennesaw Mountain Landis. Landis, for all his reputation, was not an enlightened man on racial matters.

The commissioner quickly informed Veeck that the Phillies ownership had been turned over to the National League. When Veeck asked NL president Ford Frick about buying the team, he was told it already had been sold to William Cox, a New York City lumber merchant.

"The Phillies were sold (to Cox) for about half what I had been willing to pay," said Veeck.

Cox was a George Steinbrenner 30 years before the real thing came along. He had played baseball at Yale and fancied himself an expert. He liked to hang around the clubhouse and offer advice. After one galling loss, Cox raced into the locker room and lambasted Phillies players, calling them "misfits" and "jerks."

"The only jerk around here," said manager Bucky Harris, "is the president of this ballclub."

Cox fired Harris, fomenting a revolution among Phillies

players. Harris, back in Philadelphia, told reporters that the owner had bet on Phillies games. Landis, who had won his job and fame by cracking down on gamblers, began an investigation. Cox resigned before it could be completed. When Cox soon made overtures that he wanted to get back into the game, Landis barred him for life.

◆ ◆ ◆

Robert Carpenter, a DuPont executive married to a DuPont heiress, was bemused by all of these shenanigans. He had a financial stake in a minor-league team in Wilmington, and when Cox was forced out, he figured a big-league ballclub might be a pleasant pastime for his son, Robert Jr.

The National League enthusiastically agreed with him. For $400,000, Carpenter purchased the club in November of 1943. "I think an heir has an obligation to put his money to work," Carpenter said after his father revealed him as the man who would be running the team. Getting the Phillies to work would not be so easy.

Carpenter made changes that had been standard operating procedures for most other major-league clubs. He hired accountants to crunch the numbers. He hired salesmen to sell tickets. He hired a veteran baseball man (Herb Pennock) to run the baseball operations. He poured money into a farm system that had been virtually nonexistent.

Still, the Phillies managed to do the impossible in 1947—embarrassing themselves even further. That year they were managed by Ben Chapman, a fiery Southerner who had had well publicized run-ins with Jewish fans when he played with the Yankees.

In April of that year, Jackie Robinson's rookie season, the Phillies visited Ebbets Field. Chapman and several of his play-

ers shouted racial epithets at Robinson and rode him merci-
lessly. When the Dodgers came to Philadelphia, Phillies execu-
tives urged them not to bring Robinson along. The Dodgers
ignored the request.

During warm-ups at Shibe Park, Chapman resumed his
baiting. Spotting Pee Wee Reese standing alongside the rookie,
the Phillies manager yelled, "Hey, Pee Wee! Yeah, you, Reese.
How ya like playing with a fucking nigger?"

Reese responded by putting his arm around Robinson. The
taunting ceased. Commissioner Happy Chandler later ordered
Chapman to pose with Robinson for a photo that he hoped
would demonstrate that their public war, if not their mutual
discomfort, was over.

◆ ◆ ◆

While Carpenter had the resources, that didn't always
translate into sound baseball judgment. Every organization has
its horror stories about the stars that got away. Connie Mack
had passed on a chance to sign Babe Ruth. Still, some of the
Phillies' personnel decisions could make a fan's hair stand on
end.

In 1949, they worked out a young Alabaman named Willie
Mays at Shibe Park. Somehow Carpenter and his scouts over-
looked perhaps the greatest natural gifts in baseball history. The
owner always preferred to spend his cash on pitching, and the
Phillies suggested Mays move to the mound. He soon signed
with the Giants and tormented the Phillies for more than 20
years.

Actually, the snub may have had more to do with Mays's
race than his abilities. The Phillies were woefully slow to integrate, not fielding their first black player until John Kennedy—
the quickly forgotten ballplayer, not the president—got a cup of

coffee in 1957, a decade after Robinson broke the color barrier. It wasn't until Dick Allen in 1964 that the organization would produce its first quality African-American player.

◆ ◆ ◆

During the 30 years Carpenter ran the team before turning it over to his son, Ruly, the Phillies would win just one pennant. But that championship proved to be the single event that kept the Phillies in Philadelphia and drove away the A's.

Philadelphia loved the "Whiz Kids" of 1950. The youthful, exciting team drew 1.2 million to Shibe Park in its pennant-winning season, while only 300,000 watched the last-place A's. After the 1954 season, Mack's sons sold the storied ballclub, and the A's left Philadelphia for Kansas City.

In keeping with club traditions, the 1950 Phils, with future Hall of Famers Richie Ashburn and Robin Roberts, and a Philadelphia-born slugger named Del Ennis, nearly blew the pennant. They led by 5½ games with 11 to play but didn't clinch the franchise's second NL title until the season's final day at Ebbets Field. But by then, with Curt Simmons in the Army National Guard and Bubba Church sidelined after taking a line drive in the eye, they were so short on pitching that they had to use bullpen specialist Jim Konstanty as a starter.

Konstanty was brilliant in Game 1, but the New York Yankees won 1–0. The Yankees took the next three games, too, and a city's excitement was stilled for the next 14 years.

When the 1950s ended, the Phillies were as bad as ever. Soon Ashburn and Roberts were dealt. Eddie Sawyer, the boy-wonder manager of 1950 who was brought back to try to re-bottle the Whiz Kids formula, quit one day into the 1960 season, frustrated with general manager John Quinn and the team he had provided him.

"I'm 49 years old," said Sawyer, "and I'd love to live to be 50."

Quinn hired Gene Mauch, a young, fire-breathing baseball man who liked to think he was smarter than anyone else. Philadelphia would test Mauch. His 1961 club won just 47 games, pitiful even by Phillies standards. From July 29 of that year until the second game of a doubleheader on August 20, the Phillies did not win a game, their 23 consecutive losses a major-league mark that still has not been seriously challenged.

That losing-streak-ending victory in Milwaukee precipitated another humorous moment. As the team's plane touched down in Philadelphia that night, players spotted a small crowd waiting at their gate. They were there to cheer them, as it turned out, but Phillies players being Phillies players suspected the worst.

"Get off the plane single file," instructed pitcher Frank Sullivan, "so they can't get us all with one burst."

The fans and players left the airport alive. Soon both were hibernating again. They would awake to a nightmare in the summer of 1964.

◆ ◆ ◆

Pitcher Bo Belinsky, recently acquired by the Phillies, walked into the Clearwater clubhouse on the first day of spring training in 1965. Expecting the normal locker-room banter and horseplay, he was stunned by the icy silence.

"I bounced in, looked at all my new teammates, and said, 'Hi, guys!'" Belinsky recalled. "Nothing. Not one player said a word. It was like a morgue, like someone had just died. I thought to myself, 'Whoa, what the hell has happened here?' And then I remembered . . . '64."

It is impossible to understand or appreciate the Phillies'

1980 season without understanding 1964. Certainly 1964 has plenty of company in the team's archives of despair. The 1915 and 1950 World Series. Curt Simmons's draft notice. Dick Allen's fistfight. Manny Mota's pinch-hit double off Greg Luzinski's glove in the 1977 play-offs.

But no other episode tells as much of the story of their relationship with the city's fans.

Until some team endures a more harrowing collapse—and that is nearly unimaginable—the 1964 Phillies' place in baseball legend is secure. Until then, whenever a club enters the final days of a season with a seemingly insurmountable lead, the grim drama of that Philadelphia summer will be recalled.

"What is it about 1964 and Philadelphia?" Phillies manager Jim Fregosi asked in 1993 when his team's run to a pennant was constantly interrupted by reminders of that long-ago season. "That was 30 fucking years ago! We're in first place. And that's all anybody wants to talk about."

In the spring of 1980, Paul Owens was unpacking his clothes after returning to his South Jersey home from spring training. Toward the back of the closet, he noticed a pair of suits that had been hanging there, unworn, for years. A Phillies scout at the time, Owens had bought them in September of 1964 in anticipation of his team's appearance in that year's World Series.

Every Philadelphian can recite what happened next. Twelve games left. A 6½-game lead. Chico Ruiz. Jim Bunning and Chris Short. Bunning and Short. Ten straight losses. Second place.

World Series tickets were printed, distributed, and like Owens's suits, never used.

"Damn, I felt confident," said Owens. "I was in L.A. scouting the Dodgers, and I went out and bought two new suits on credit. I couldn't afford them, but I wanted to make sure I looked neat at the World Series. During the losing streak, scouts from other teams would ask me, 'What's with you guys? You aren't going to blow this thing, are you?' I'd tell them we would win the next game and clinch real soon. But we never could do it. Never could win that one lousy game we needed. . . . And you know, I always hated those suits."

The 1964 Phillies were not the best team in the National League. They may not even have been the sixth best. But they should have won the pennant. In most cases, a 6½-game lead with 12 to play is sufficient to accomplish that.

On September 20, 1964, the Phillies flew home from the West Coast with a 6½-game lead. Philadelphia was giddy with World Series fever. Mayor James Tate had met the team's plane at the airport. World Series ticket information filled the papers. "Go, Go Phillies!" played on the radio. Phillies wives talked openly about how many tickets they needed for out-of-town family and friends.

Then, the following night, with future Hall of Famer Frank Robinson at bat in a scoreless game, Cincinnati's Chico Ruiz inexplicably broke for home.

He made it. The Phillies would not.

Ruiz's mad dash with one of baseball's best hitters at the plate defied logic. For the Phillies, for nearly two more painful weeks, nothing would make sense again.

Mauch figured he needed only another win or two, and he tried to steal them by pitching Bunning and Short without their normal rest. Suddenly Allen and Johnny Callison, who had carried the team all year, couldn't hit with men on base. And when the previously dependable bullpen did get a lead to hold, it couldn't.

The Reds won the Ruiz game 1–0 and swept the Phillies. So did the Braves. Glad to escape the boos and the questions, they left Connie Mack Stadium for St. Louis. The Cardinals, seeing fear in their eyes, swept them, too.

"They came to St. Louis with a 1½-game lead, and they left trailing us by that same margin," said Cardinals shortstop Dick Groat. "We swept them. They were tight, real tight. I watched them before the game, and you could almost feel how tight they were. You couldn't help but notice it—even during the warm-ups."

Philadelphia lost the opener in the season-ending series in Cincinnati to run its deadly losing streak to ten. They won the next two days, but it was too late. The St. Louis Cardinals took the pennant with a final-day victory in New York.

The greatest wreck in baseball history was complete.

As Belinsky noted the following spring, that season never went away. Phillies players carried the choke label like an albatross. The cursed Mauch, though he would come agonizingly close twice more with the California Angels, never made it to a World Series. The organization, desperate to forget the nightmare, made a spate of ill-conceived deals that haunted the team for another decade.

Worst of all, Phillies fans, who had always attributed the franchise's historic misfortune to frugality and bad players, now were convinced some malevolent force was at work.

"It hurt," said Owens, "and it hurt for a long time. No one wanted to believe it. I don't think a lot of the fans realized it at the time, but it was something they would never really be able to shake . . . like a great big cloud hanging over the city."

Fans were stunned. What little trust they had was shattered. They always had been negative and boo-happy, but after 1964 their attitudes grew even darker. It was after the Phillies collapse that they drove Eagles coach Joe Kuharich out of town—and nearly to a nervous breakdown—that they booed Santa Claus and pelted him with snowballs, that they prompted Allen to scribble desperate messages, pleading for a trade, in the first-base dirt.

"I remember sitting out on the porch with my dad in the dark," said Joe Kerrigan, a native Philadelphian and now the Boston Red Sox pitching coach. "We would be listening to the Phillies games during that long losing streak, and he would be cussing and moaning about some of Mauch's moves. When they finally blew it, he lost a lot of love in his heart for the Phillies. And he never got it back."

Chapter 2

As Welcome as a Rose in May

We flubbed that dub a little bit.

DANNY OZARK, 1978

Ruly Carpenter, Yale graduate, semipro pitcher, was 32 when his father handed him the team on November 22, 1972. In some ways, the transition couldn't have come at a better time for him.

Veterans Stadium was less than two years old, and its modern amenities made it, for a brief time anyway, a showplace. Phillies fans, tired of navigating the decaying neighborhood around Connie Mack Stadium, flocked to the South Philadelphia facility and its acres of parking lots. Once inside, they were getting excited about youngsters like Schmidt, Boone, Luzinski, and Bowa.

On the other hand, building labor strife clouded Carpenter's horizon. The game's economics were changing, the Players Association's strength was growing, and most of the owners were stubbornly clinging to the past.

Just that winter, the elder Carpenter had met with the Phillies player representatives, Tim McCarver and Terry Harmon. He told them baseball had always been successful without

Marvin Miller. Why didn't they just push their union chief aside and get back to doing business in the old-fashioned way? Miller told McCarver to end the meetings. "They're doing more harm than good," Miller said.

Being a player rep was a perilous duty in those days. Owners viewed them as ingrates, troublemakers. Between the end of the 1971 season and the brief strike before the 1972 season, 16 of the 24 player reps were traded or released.

The Phillies' young owner figured the issues soon would move beyond the pension contributions and petty grievances that concerned both sides now. He wasn't sure what form the trouble would take, but it was out there, not far away.

Bob Carpenter had insisted his son take a working tour of the organization. Time in the minor leagues convinced Ruly that scouting and development were essential if the Phillies were ever going to be anything but laughingstocks.

Owens had been the young Carpenter's mentor. They were a team, moving up through the organization in tandem. The elder Carpenter hoped Owens would do for his son what his first general manager, Herb Pennock, had done for him—win him a pennant. So when Owens got the GM's job, on June 3, 1972, the changeover in ownership seemed inevitable. Five months later it came.

Owens had replaced John Quinn, a gruff man whose failings will forever be overshadowed by the last trade he made.

Steve Carlton, always as independent-minded as he was talented, had been wrestling Cardinals owner Augie Busch over a new contract. Busch, already upset by the economic changes then beginning to unfold, demanded Carlton be dealt.

He didn't come cheaply. Quinn, with considerable input from Owens, sent St. Louis Rick Wise, a quality pitcher whose no-hitter (in a game in which he also homered twice) had been one of the few bright spots in the previous Phillies season. It was no coincidence that Wise, too, was a holdout.

The Phillies would win 59 games in 1972. Carlton won 27 of them.

In that same season, Schmidt and Boone were called up in September. Owens and Green saw that—along with Luzinski, Bowa, and Carlton—they gave the Phillies a potential nucleus. Owens, in fact, saw it firsthand. In July, he fired Frank Lucchesi and went into the dugout himself.

"I learned a lot," said Owens of his managing stint. "I heard and saw things in the dugout I couldn't possibly have known if I hadn't been in uniform. I found out that there were six or seven guys we could build around."

That winter speculation over a new manager turned to Richie Ashburn, Jim Bunning, and former Reds manager Dave Bristol. Bunning interviewed with Carpenter and Owens and believed he was the front-runner. So did Bristol.

Instead, impressed with his Dodgers connections, the Phillies hired Danny Ozark, a little-known L.A. coach. Carpenter realized Ozark was virtually unknown in Philadelphia, but his Dodgers background indicated he'd stress fundamentals and lay an easy hand on this young team.

Ozark was a nice, beagle-faced man who was as ill suited to Philadelphia as Philadelphia Orchestra conductor Eugene Ormandy would have been with the Rolling Stones. When Philadelphians pictured a baseball manager in 1977, they still thought of Mauch.

Managers, in their view, were flinty-eyed little sons of bitches who loved nothing better than the cerebral chess matches baseball games often became. They were passionate enough to overturn a buffet table following a loss or kick an umpire's shin. They were tough, edgy, and smart—three qualities no one would ever attribute to the phlegmatic Ozark.

Asked at his introductory news conference how he had reacted to the news that, after all these years in the game, he at last had become a big-league manager, Ozark practically yawned.

"I wasn't overly excited," he said. "I didn't jump and say, 'Whoopee!'"

Neither did Phillies fans. But in Ozark's defense, Philadelphia managers traditionally didn't win very often, and he would.

The Phillies were lousy and last again in 1973, and Ozark very nearly lost his job. On June 1, during a series in Los Angeles, several players went to the GM's room. Like Luther en route to Wittenberg, they carried a long list of grievances. Ozark was clueless, they said. He knew nothing about pitchers, often botched in-game strategy, and had lost control of his clubhouse.

They pleaded with Owens to come back to the dugout as he had done the previous season.

"I know there are problems," Owens told them. "That's why I'm making these road trips. But I've got to find out for myself. Go out there and hang in there tough and show me you're professionals."

Later that year, he needed the same advice himself. Following a pair of one-sided losses in Montreal, Owens told a reporter in a hotel bar that Ozark "had failed to establish a rapport, a line of communication with his players. . . . He's got three weeks."

He survived almost another six years. The Phillies finished last again in 1973, their 71–91 record the third worst in the major leagues. For all his garbled syntax and baffling maneuvers, Ozark had managed two significant accomplishments that first year. He stuck with Boone and Schmidt all season. Boone was fine. The catcher played in 145 games, hit .261 with 10 homers and 61 RBIs. Schmidt, though, looked overmatched.

His season-ending average of .196 was an embarrassment. He struck out 136 times in 367 at bats. But he also hit 18 homers and played third base marvelously.

"This kid's gonna be a hell of a player," said Ozark. "Anyone can see that he's got a bright future."

The same couldn't be said for the manager. Conlin's postseason review of the team summed up how players and Philadelphians felt about "The Wizard of Oze": "What surfaced was a man who had none of (Gene) Mauch's current tactical brilliance and all of Gene's early inability to communicate with young players. His conduct of a ballgame showed the inconsistency of the born hunch player, mixing whim with baseball logic, prestidigitation with percentages."

But the nucleus was maturing. The Phillies jumped from sixth to third in 1974. Philadelphia's fans, their hopes buoyed by second baseman Dave Cash's "Yes We Can" slogan, were reappearing in record numbers. They drew a franchise record 1.8 million in 1974, 1.9 million in 1975 when they finished second to the Pirates.

By then the Phillies believed they were winning despite Ozark. Most of the players liked the manager personally, but he had lost their respect as a disciplinarian and a game tactician.

"If you listened to them," Frank Dolson said 20 years later, "you'd wonder how the Phillies managed to win three straight division titles. In their view, Ozark obviously was someone who couldn't lead a thirsty horse to water."

Whenever Bowa lobbied for Ozark's ouster, which was increasingly often as the years went by, he liked to use a play during the 1978 season as evidence.

With Bowa at third and Jerry Martin at first, Ozark signaled for a double steal. This was odd because there were two outs and the count on batter Jose Cardenal was 0–2. With two strikes, Cardenal had to swing if the pitch were close.

Ozark assumed Mets pitcher Paul Siebert, a left-hander, would throw to first when he saw Martin take off. Bowa then would scamper home easily. Why he assumed that was anyone's guess. Anyway, Martin took off. And Bowa took off. And Siebert threw a perfect strike.

Bowa was about ten feet from Cardenal when the hitter lined a foul ball into the seats.

"It is dangerous. Very, very dangerous," Cardenal said of the play. "I would hate to be that guy at third base."

Ozark took the blame as only the malaprop-prone manager could. "We flubbed that dub a little bit," he said.

The manager permanently cemented his image as a know-nothing at the end of the 1975 season. On September 22, after a victory gave the Pirates a fourth NL East title in five years, he was asked what remained to be accomplished by his second-place Phils.

"We'll try to win tomorrow," he said. "We're not out of it yet."

Told the Phillies trailed by seven games and, like Pittsburgh, had only six to play, Ozark appeared stunned. "Well, that's news to me," he said. "That's very disheartening."

Earlier that month, as the Phillies foundered behind the Pirates, the *Daily News* ran a poll asking readers who ought to manage. "Super Team" Ashburn, then a broadcaster with the team, won by a landslide. Ozark finished far back in the pack.

◆ ◆ ◆

Owens made two wonderful moves in 1975, as significant as any in the Phillies march to a world championship. Before the season, he got McGraw from the Mets. Then, in May, he acquired centerfielder Maddox from the San Francisco Giants for Willie Montanez, a flashy former Rookie of the Year.

A year later, in 1976, the Phillies set a franchise record with

101 victories in winning their first NL East title. Their signature game came on April 17 at Wrigley Field. That Saturday afternoon, with Carlton knocked out early, they overcame deficits of 12–1 and 13–2. Schmidt homered four times, the last in the tenth inning, in an 18–16 victory. Around the country, Philadelphia again began to surface on the radar screens of baseball fans.

"Philadelphia gets the All-Star Game this month," wrote Red Smith in July of that year. "The Phillies' Robin Roberts will be inducted into the Hall of Fame in August. And when we speak of the Bicentennial, we're talking about Philadelphia because that's where this nation started.

"Bicentennials come once in 200 years. Pennants come oftener in Betsy Ross's town, but not much."

Schmidt's four-homer game sent the Phillies into the longest run of excellent baseball any fan could recall. They led the Pirates by 15½ games in late August. But, Philadelphia being Philadelphia, two weeks later that lead had dwindled to 5½ games. All of sudden, the specter of 1964 was resurrected. Talk of the infamous collapse filled the radio shows, the newspapers, the taverns.

"Nineteen sixty-four is a thing of the past," said the always optimistic Cash. "You bury the past."

Not in Philadelphia. The talk intensified. Bobby Wine, a shortstop in 1964 and now a Phils coach, asked Ozark if he could speak to the team.

"This club has a lot more talent than we had then," Wine said. "We had two guys playing regularly—Allen and Callison. The rest of us were platoon players, part-time players. . . . You're the Phillies of this year, not 1964."

They finally gathered themselves and won the division easily. Again, it all meant nothing. The powerful Reds swept them in the NLCS, and their postseason losing streak stretched to 11.

Watching the Phillies from across the field in the series, Rose mentioned to teammate Joe Morgan that "that team's got a lot of talent. All they need is a leader."

There was something both comfortable and unpleasant about that Phillies team and the championship clubs that would follow in 1977 and 1978. Having come through the system together, they were very close and yet very distant.

"Bowa, Boone, Schmidt, Luzinski, those guys knew each other so well," said Owens. "They'd ride each other if one wasn't pulling his weight. I remember when Bowa and Luzinski would see some of the things Schmidt said in the papers, they'd get all over him. 'How could you say something that stupid?' That sort of thing."

But the tightness led to jealousies.

"Bowa was afraid Boonie would get more hits than him," said Rose. "Schmitty didn't want Bull to get more homers than him. Bull didn't want Schmitty to get more ink than him. There was a lot of that."

After 1976, the players knew they were stuck with Ozark. The *Sporting News* named him Manager of the Year on October 13. The next day he signed a two-year extension.

"I think everyone has known Danny was coming back," said Owens, apparently forgetting his barroom conversation a few months earlier. "There was never any doubt in my mind."

The Pirates won 96 games in 1977—and finished 5½ games behind. The Phillies recorded 101 victories for a second straight season. Luzinski had his best year with 39 homers and 130 RBIs. Schmidt had 38 homers and 114 runs scored. The Phillies' average was a league-best .279. Carlton led the majors with 23 victories, had a 2.64 ERA, and won another Cy Young Award. Larry Christenson, just 23, added 19. Only Cincinnati committed fewer errors.

Owens had brought in Ted Sizemore from L.A. to play second and left-handed-hitting Richie Hebner, a former Pirate, to play first. His bench, with veterans like Ollie Brown, Jay Johnstone, and Davey Johnson, was deep.

At midseason, he stole another disgruntled star from St. Louis, acquiring Bake McBride for Tom Underwood, Dane Iorg, and Rick Bosetti. McBride's bushy Afro and beard upset Cardinals manager Vern Rapp when the outfielder arrived early at spring training. Rapp told him to get a haircut and shave. McBride said he'd wait. He got to Philadelphia before a barber's chair. After riding the bench in St. Louis, McBride hit .339 in 85 games with the Phillies and stole 27 bases.

"There's no question that the 1977 team was the best in baseball and the best Phillies team in a long time," said Owens. "We had the top defense in the league. We had a great lineup. We had guys on the bench like Ollie Brown and Jay Johnstone who could step in and play for a few days, and not just fill in but really contribute. The starting pitching, with Carlton and Jim Lonborg and Jim Kaat, was deeper and more experienced than 1980. And the bullpen was tremendous with Tug, (Warren) Brusstar, and Garber."

Owens forgot Martin, an excellent defensive outfielder and decent pinch hitter. When Ozark forgot about him, too, the wonderful season of 1977 would end in yet another disappointment.

This time the Phillies split the first two games of the NLCS with the Dodgers in L.A. As they flew back to Philadelphia on October 6, 1977, the city's fans were beginning to believe that maybe this was the year their parents told them would never come.

The next afternoon, their minds were changed, their hearts broken again.

◆ ◆ ◆

Philadelphians call it "Black Friday" now, but it really was a sparkling autumn afternoon.

The Phillies were trailing 2–0 in the second inning when Dodgers starter Burt Hooton lost control of his pitches and himself. At one point, disputing a pitch, the Texan gestured angrily toward the home-plate umpire. Big mistake. Sniffing blood, the 63,719 fans came to their feet.

Each subsequent pitch was accompanied by louder and louder hooting. As the balls and the walks piled up, the stadium rumbled with noise. Fans watching ABC's broadcast at home had difficulty hearing Howard Cosell amid the bellowing—not necessarily a bad thing, as many pointed out.

"I don't think I've ever heard noise like that," said Bowa. "They hooted the guy right off the mound."

Hooton walked four straight batters, and the Phils had a 3–2 lead. They were in front 5–3 to start the ninth, an inning that would encapsulate a century of Phillies misery.

Gene Garber retired L.A.'s first two hitters. But pinch hitter Vic Davalillo beat out a marvelous drag bunt. Some fans, hoarse but still happy, noticed that Ozark, who almost always replaced Luzinski with Martin when he had a late-inning lead, had left the big leftfielder out there. If you were a real Philadelphian, you sensed what would happen next.

Pinch hitter Manny Mota, with two strikes on him and the crowd standing and screaming, slapped an inside fastball to deep left. Luzinski retreated, got a step from the wall, and leaped. The ball kicked off his glove, hit the wall, and fell back into his mitt. When Luzinski gathered it in, his hurried throw eluded the cutoff man, allowing Davalillo to score and Mota to advance to third.

"He was the third batter up in the ninth," Ozark explained later about Luzinski's staying put, as much as admitting he hadn't managed to protect a lead because he had been too worried about losing it. "I wanted him in the lineup in case the game was tied."

Soon it would be.

Davey Lopes batted next. Fearing his speed, and already burned by Davalillo, Schmidt moved up a few steps at third.

"I was afraid with the tying run on, he might try to bunt his way on," said Schmidt.

Lopes lashed a ball right at him. It caromed off Schmidt's glove on a line to Bowa. The shortstop vacuumed it up and fired to first. Lopes appeared to be out, but Bruce Froemming signaled safe. The score was tied as first baseman Hebner and Ozark went after the umpire.

"If he had called the play right, both me and Hebner would have been thrown out," said Ozark. "He didn't know what the fuck to call it, so he called it safe. He was stunned by Bowa's throw as far as I'm concerned. He just anticipated Bowa couldn't make the throw. He's got his hands stuffed in his pockets half the fucking time."

The weight of Phillies history had squeezed all the air out of the giant stadium. Garber's pickoff throw was wild, pushing Lopes into scoring position. Bill Russell's game-winning RBI single was a foregone conclusion.

So was Game 4. On a gloomy, rainy Saturday night, Tommy John outpitched Carlton. The Dodgers won the game 4–1, the series 3–1.

"Death had come to the executioners," wrote Conlin. "The Phillies had met the enemy, and it was them."

◆ ◆ ◆

A year later, the same two teams met again in the NLCS. This time the Phillies had scuffled to get there, winning just 90 games and nearly blowing a late-season lead to the Pirates.

Trailing the Phils by 10½ games in mid-August, Pittsburgh won 22 of 25 and when the Phillies came to Three Rivers Stadium for a four-game series on the final weekend, their lead was just 3½ games. The Pirates closed even further by winning Friday night's double header, their 23rd and 24th straight home victories.

Then on Saturday, they grabbed an instant lead when Willie Stargell hit a first-inning grand slam off Randy Lerch. But Lerch would homer twice himself, and Luzinski added a monstrous three-run homer in the Phillies' 10–8 division clincher.

Phillies pitchers, despite Owens's midseason reacquisition of Dick Ruthven from Atlanta (for Garber), led the league in walks (393) and opponents' on-base percentage (.305). Carlton slumped to 16–13. Christenson fell from 19–6 to 13–14.

Offensively, Schmidt, who suffered several leg injuries, hit just 21 homers and drove in 78—his lowest totals since 1973. Luzinski had another solid year, but even his numbers dipped —35 home runs, 101 RBIs.

The Dodgers took the first two NLCS games in Philadelphia. That meant that of the 11 postseason games the Phillies had played at home, they had won just once. Carlton got them a victory in Game 3 in Los Angeles. But Game 4 and the series ended soon after Maddox dropped Dusty Baker's two-out, tenth-inning line drive.

"I guess," said Ozark, "all the bad things happen to the good guys."

Owens went into that off-season wanting a second baseman. Sizemore was aging and had lost considerable range—a mortal sin on Astroturf. He pried Manny Trillo from the Cubs along with Greg Gross for Martin, Sizemore, Barry Foote, Derek Bothelo, and Henry Mack.

Trillo, a Venezuelan, had originally been signed by the Phillies as a 17-year-old catcher. His first minor-league manager, at Huron of the Northern League, was Dallas Green, who switched the physically fragile catcher to second base. In 1969, the Phillies left him unprotected, and the Oakland A's stole Trillo away.

That move, thought Owens, ought to do it. "I liked our chances again with that lineup."

Then, as the off-season progressed, he learned that Pete Rose wanted out of Cincinnati.

◆ ◆ ◆

Several players, including Bowa and Schmidt, urged Carpenter to take a run at the Reds' hit machine.

Rose and Reds GM Dick Wagner were feuding. Rose wanted a big raise from the $365,000-a-year deal that expired after the 1978 season. He was a hometown hero who had more than 3,000 hits. He had helped the Reds win four pennants and two World Series. A nice raise shouldn't have been a problem.

But Rose's negotiations with Wagner in 1976 had been bitter. Now Wagner took his player's demands personally. He told Rose the kind of money he sought was impossible. Things got ugly and when the Reds took out a newspaper advertisement pleading their case, Rose told his agent, Reuven Katz, to look elsewhere.

Immediately, Atlanta, Pittsburgh, St. Louis, Kansas City, and Philadelphia expressed interest. The self-proclaimed "most famous white athlete in America," Rose was a tough negotiator. He always had a mercenary side that contradicted a playing style that suggested he'd perform for nothing. His half-million dollar personal endorsement deal with Mizuno, a Japanese sporting goods company, was risky at a time when American workers felt threatened by Japan. But it broke new ground for professional athletes.

Carpenter, despite a fortune estimated then at $330 million, was a reluctant participant. The Phillies owner despised free agency. He had predicted it would result in championships going to the highest bidders. Sure enough, George Steinbrenner's Yankees, with celebrated free agents Catfish Hunter and Reggie Jackson, won the new era's first two World Series in 1977 and 1978.

"If he had failed," Carpenter lamented later, "I don't think you'd see what you do today."

Atlanta offered $1 million a year, but Rose didn't want to go to a loser and he hated playing to the tiny crowds the Braves regularly drew to Fulton County Stadium. Kansas City matched the Braves and added some stock in Ewing Kauffman's pharmaceutical companies.

St. Louis bid less, but Augie Busch promised Budweiser riches. Pittsburgh's offer really tempted Rose, a horseplayer, because it included interest in some of owners John and Dan Galbreath's thoroughbreds.

The Phillies were last on Rose's tour. He had planned it that way. Rose loved Philadelphia's spirited baseball atmosphere. He was close to guys like Bowa, Schmidt, and Luzinski and believed he could win them the pennant that had eluded them the last three years.

"I'm not bragging, but I was exactly what they needed," he said. "Ask anybody who watched that team. I was a perfect fit. They needed a leader. Those guys were always arguing among themselves. They were a little jealous. They'd compare stats. I got there and said, 'Hey, take one look at my stats and shut up.'"

Carpenter was ready with a $2.1 million, three-year package when Rose visited his Delaware estate for lunch. Katz told him how much the other offers were worth. Rose would be willing to play in Philadelphia for less—but not that much less. The Phillies owner blanched, and the meeting ended.

Phillies VP Bill Giles, the son of ex-NL president Warren Giles, intervened. He appealed to Rose's sense of history. "Stay in our league," he told him, "and you'll break Stan Musial's National League hit record in a couple of years. By the time you're done, you'll have more league records than anyone."

The point scored. Katz suggested Rose would reconsider if the Phillies would "get creative."

The Phillies already drew two million fans. Rose likely would help the gate but not enough to pay for the payroll bump his signing would create. Carpenter had the money. He had given Schmidt a six-year, $3.36 million contract in 1977. But he wasn't going to spend it on a 37-year-old free agent developed in another organization. The hell if he'd become another Steinbrenner.

Giles thought immediately about TV. He arranged a meeting with the team's flagship station, WPHL-TV. The Phillies and WPHL had just signed a new deal. Rose, Giles pointed out, would mean increased ratings. The station agreed to renegotiate. They upped their annual fee to $1.9 million, an increase of $600,000.

Now the Phils offered Rose $800,000 a season for four years. That, Rose knew, was exactly what pro sport's highest-paid player, David Thompson of the NBA's Denver Nuggets, earned. "Make it $805,000," he said, "and I'm there."

The signing instantly cleared up some of the Phillies' personality problems.

"In my opinion, if Mike Schmidt had a shortcoming, it was that he didn't realize how good he was," said Owens. "Pete had a lot to do with changing that."

For Schmidt, whom Rose called "Herbie," the next three seasons would be the best of a great career, cementing himself as a future Hall of Famer. He won two MVP Awards, hit 124 home runs, and knocked in 326 runs (despite a strike-shortened 1981 season).

"Bowa loved him, too," said Owens. "Pete, for all he had accomplished, set a good example for those guys. He was the first guy in the clubhouse every day. He'd get there at 1:30 (for a 7:35 game), go through his mail, get himself ready."

And Rose was the in-your-face, more-heart-than-talent type Phillies fans loved. Now who could say this team had no guts? Very quickly, the Phillies season-ticket sales jumped by $2.5 million.

The funk created by a third-straight play-off elimination lifted overnight.

◆ ◆ ◆

With Rose and Trillo, the lineup that would win the Phillies a World Series was complete. Fans, players, and club officials expected a championship in 1979.

The Phillies started rapidly that year and after Schmidt's tenth-inning homer won a 23–22 game at Wrigley on May 17, they were a gaudy 24–10 with a four-game lead. Soon, however, a long run of injuries began. As the disabled list's population swelled, their record slipped.

Back home after Chicago, they were swept by Montreal. They couldn't put a three-game win streak together until July 4. By then the Phillies were just one game over .500 and in fifth place.

It wasn't Rose's fault. He not only attracted fans, he had a terrific season on the field. The Phillies found a position for him—his fourth in the big leagues—by moving first baseman Hebner to the Mets for Nino Espinosa, who would win 14 games for them in 1979.

Ozark, gilding his infamous reputation further, wasn't crazy about adding Rose. Hebner, who had 35 homers and 133 RBIs in his two Philadelphia seasons, had given him some left-handed power to stick between Schmidt and Luzinski.

All Rose did was field like a veteran first baseman, hit .331, collect 208 hits, and steal a career-high 20 bases. In September, while the rest of the club struggled to accommodate Green, he hit .421 to win the NL's Player of the Month award.

Imagine how he might have performed if his marriage hadn't been publicly disintegrating that summer and if a *Playboy* interview hadn't backfired. The men's magazine quoted Rose as saying he had taken "greenies," amphetamines—an admission that would be resurrected with great interest the following summer.

Schmidt, his self-doubts eased by Rose's presence, set a Phillies record with 45 home runs. Bowa established a major-league mark by committing just six errors, but somehow didn't win a Gold Glove. Four of his teammates—Trillo, Boone, Maddox, and Schmidt—did. Philadelphia was the equal to anyone up the middle.

"That's the thing about those Phillies teams that a lot of people don't mention," said Del Unser. "Their defense might have been their strongest attribute."

It certainly wasn't their bones and ligaments. Rose was the only regular who didn't go down that year. Trillo missed 46 games with a broken arm. Boone missed 23 with a broken finger and then a bad knee that required surgery. Luzinski, heavier than ever, missed 26 games with various leg ailments. Bowa was out 16 games with a thumb injury.

On July 4, they lost three starting pitchers quicker than you could say "Ball Four." Ruthven and Christenson went on the disabled list, and Lerch, a left-hander, had suffered a broken right wrist when he was mugged in downtown Philadelphia. Ruthven and Christenson, counted on to be the Nos. 2 and 3 starters behind Carlton, combined for 39 starts and just 12 victories.

"We're playing Class D baseball," Ozark said in July.

At last, Philadelphians thought, Ozark had brought the Phillies down to his level.

The record crowds at the Vet became angry Greek choruses, sounding a vociferous valedictory for the manager and, they hoped, several of his players. Eventually, the manager couldn't pop his head out of the dugout without inciting the fans. Luzinski, too, his waistline expanding, became a favorite target.

Contenders hovered over the Phillies' talent-rich roster like vultures late that summer. Owens had made an unsuccessful run at Texas's Sparky Lyle. The Rangers, according to Carpenter, also initiated a blockbuster megadeal that he had to veto over the objections of his baseball people.

"I didn't want to do it," he said. "(If they had,) [w]e would not have had three of the stars of the 1980 team."

The season was embarrassing enough for the league's highest-paid team, but the players and manager seemed intent on making it worse. Ozark had alienated much of the team, particularly its pitchers. Veterans like McGraw and Carlton didn't think the manager understood the first thing about handling a staff. McGraw often complained about inactivity. And if Carlton wanted to come out of a game, he'd let the manager know, not the other way around.

On June 30, in St. Louis, when Ozark pulled him, Carlton petulantly spiked the ball at his manager's feet. Ozark fined him and fumed.

"The guy tried to show me up out there," he said, "and I'm damned upset about it."

One night in Cincinnati, Ozark hit Carlton eighth. The pitcher killed one rally by rolling into a double play. Later he struck out with the go-ahead run at second. The following afternoon, in a nationally televised game, Ozark's lineup shocked his players. He put Boone and Schmidt at their old college positions, third and short. Bud Harrelson was at second and McCarver behind the plate.

"I don't mind breaking out my old high school position in front of a small crowd, but the whole nation will be watching," said Schmidt.

On August 7, Ozark pinch-hit Gross for Luzinski with the bases loaded. Afterward, he hinted to sportswriters that he was either going to quit or be fired. Still, nothing happened. By then, the mutineers reigned. Everyone but Charles Goren was playing bridge, or rummy, or hearts in the clubhouse. Players ignored infield practice and belittled their manager when he was within earshot.

Finally, on August 31, Ozark was summoned to Owens's Atlanta hotel room. Every baseball fan in America could have told him what was about to happen. Newspapers in every city the Phillies visited trumpeted his imminent firing. Vet fans chanted "Oze Must Go!" Yet, a dunderhead to the end, Ozark said he never saw it coming.

"I thought it was probably to go over the waiver list, something like that," he said. "I went upstairs thinking, 'Well, when are we bringing the (minor-league) guys up from Oklahoma City?' But Paul just told me, 'We're going to make a change.' I was stunned."

Somehow a manager who had compiled a seven-year record of 594–510 and won three division titles had left town as a buffoon. That was Philadelphia. Losing with a bad team was one thing. Frank Lucchesi could out-malaprop Ozark. And his teams finished last. Yet no one called for his head on a Louisville Slugger. But when the city finally got a team capable of winning a World Series, it demanded more from a manager than Ozark ever displayed.

Carpenter later said the firing was the most difficult decision he had to make in his nine years as owner. His mind was made up, he said, during a late-August homestand when the Phillies slipped below .500 for the first time that season.

"We had a dreadful homestand, losing eight of nine games to Atlanta, Houston, and Cincinnati. We were beginning to lose our fans, too," Carpenter explained to *Wilmington News-Journal* beat writer Hal Bodley for his book, *The Team That Wouldn't Die.* "We waited for the team to go to Atlanta before we made the announcement because I didn't want a three-ring media circus. Danny deserved better than that."

"If Danny Ozark had one fault it was that he was too damn nice," said Carpenter. "He was tremendously loyal to his players. There were just times when he should have been a hell of a lot tougher on those guys and really chewed their butts out or fined them or done whatever a manager should do. On the other hand, he was a very tough person to put up with the things he did, the crap he took."

While the Phillies felt a sense of relief that day, there were many times in the next 14 months when they would have welcomed back Ozark.

His replacement came in barking and challenging. The players didn't know it yet, but Green had a mandate from Carpenter and Owens to get tough with them. As soon as he opened his mouth during a team meeting that afternoon of

August 31, they understood toughness wouldn't be a problem for their new manager.

"The Phillies didn't fire Danny Ozark," Green told them. "You guys fired Danny Ozark."

He told them he was going to use the last month of the season to find out who wanted to play and who didn't. He implied some of the veterans had been loafing, and several of them resented that.

"I had spent all summer giving it everything I had," said Maddox, "and to have the manager say that, I guess I took it personally."

Green immediately suggested that this team needed a good, swift kick in the attitude.

"I'm an attitude guy," he said. "I don't think you can accomplish anything if you don't have the right attitude."

Green later said that "if there's going to be any bitching, I wanted it all directed at me."

He couldn't have imagined how successful he would be in accomplishing that.

◆ ◆ ◆

Few people saw Green as a solution to the Phillies' horrible past. By the start of the 1980 season, sportswriters and even their own fans were writing them off.

Following the 1978 play-off disaster, best-selling author James Michener, a suburban Philadelphia resident and lifelong Phils fan, had written an op-ed piece for the *New York Times* that discussed the futility of rooting for the Phillies.

"A young literary critic asked me the other day: 'Mr. Michener, you seem to be optimistic about the human race. Don't you have a sense of tragedy?'" Michener wrote. "I thought a minute and told him: 'Young man, when you root for the Phillies, you acquire a sense of tragedy.'

"Marvin (a Michener friend and fellow Phillies fan) must have been thinking of this when he handed me a slip of paper to be used in case he died before me. On his tombstone he wants:

"'Here lies a Phillies Phan, still hoping for that one great year.'"

Hold on, Marvin, it was coming.

Chapter 3

 # The Pope's Puzzle Comes Together

These two halves of God—the Pope and the Emperor.
VICTOR HUGO, *HERNANI*

Paul Owens and his tumbler of Jack Daniels were alone at the bar in the San Francisco Hilton. On this night, he had business to conduct and this was his office.

The Phillies general manager had grown up in the baseball generation for whom the hotel bar was sacred ground. There, in the smoky hours between midnight and closing time, trades were completed, managers fired, big-league careers begun and ended.

Sure there were plenty of ugly stories about bars. About Billy Martin's brawls, about on-the-road trysts that ended marriages, about near fights and liquor-induced threats. But more often than not in baseball, alcohol lubricated the rough business of negotiations, eased the bad news, soothed raw tempers.

In the early morning hours of September 1, 1980, the bourbon wasn't doing a damn thing for Owens. He'd been upset ever since he had watched the Phillies lose 10–3 to the Padres in San Diego earlier that day.

Somehow, despite all the bickering, bitching, and newspaper headlines, the Phillies had remained in the middle of the NL East race. They were just a half-game behind Montreal and Pittsburgh with a month to go. But every time it looked like they were ready to put a run together, somebody made a stupid mistake or shot off his mouth. Some of those misplays he saw in San Diego, there was no excuse for them.

Owens lit another cigarette and recalled them now.

Early in the game, Maddox chased a high fly ball into right-center. The GM instinctively relaxed. Maddox, a five-time Gold Glove winner, was as sure a thing as there was in baseball. This time, though, the Philadelphia centerfielder looked to be having trouble locating the ball. He squinted and raised his right hand to his eyes, shielding them from the sun.

"Where the hell are his sunglasses?" Owens muttered to himself.

It wasn't like this was April in Chicago. This was a day game in August in San Diego! The sun never stopped shining there. And every outfielder in the league knew there was a bad glare in right-center at Jack Murphy Stadium.

Maddox, his sunglasses in his back pocket, got a glove on the ball, but dropped it.

A few innings later, another ball was hit to nearly the same spot. Owens watched Maddox again move haltingly toward it.

"Jesus Christ!" the GM yelled this time, startling his wife, Marcelle, who had accompanied him on the West Coast trip. "He still isn't wearing sunglasses!"

This ball fell in, too. Owens's face turned the color of the Phillies' hats.

"To me," Maddox would explain after the game, "I can play just as well without sunglasses."

Owens still hadn't relaxed when Ozzie Smith bounced a slow roller to the shortstop. Bowa, quick and strong-armed, might have been the best in the league on those plays. The little guy could be a pain in the ass, Owens thought, but he made all the plays. All last year, he committed only six errors—phenomenal for a shortstop.

Now, however, Bowa hesitated on his charge, finally backing up. Smith beat his hurried throw easily.

"God dammit!" yelled Owens. "It almost looks like he's playing cautious, worried about messing up some damn defensive record."

When the 10–3 defeat was over and the Phillies had missed an opportunity to move into first place, Owens thought about going right into the clubhouse and airing out his frustration. But experience had taught him it often was better to wait, to be patient. Sometimes glaring mistakes became understandable errors with the passage of time. He'd hold off. Maybe that would calm him down.

It didn't.

The team left for San Francisco and just before the Phillies charter touched down, Owens told Green he wanted to talk.

"As soon as you get to the hotel and check in, come to my room," Owens told him.

Twenty years later, in semiretirement, Owens still recalled his room number at the Hilton.

"It was 413. I'll never forget that."

While his wife waited for him downstairs in the restaurant, Owens and Green talked.

"I said, 'Dallas, I don't go down into the clubhouse much. But god dammit, I want a meeting. And I want it before tomorrow's game.'"

Owens, nicknamed "Pope" because of his uncanny resemblance to Pope Paul VI, joined his wife, and they had a quiet—very quiet—dinner. Then he excused himself and headed for the bar. Green and some of his coaches soon joined him there. In the unwritten but byzantine code governing baseball behavior, the hotel bar belonged to the manager and club officials. Because of that, sportswriters tended to gravitate there as well. Ballplayers drank elsewhere.

On this night, the traveling party had checked in early enough to permit several players to head into downtown San Francisco, just a short cab ride away. Carlton had taken a group of pitchers and McCarver to a tony restaurant with a long wine list.

Owens and Green commiserated over their drinks. Neither man thought they ought to be dealing with fundamentals problems like these on a veteran-heavy ballclub. Not on August 31. Maybe they had been wrong. Maybe the writers were right and this homegrown nucleus—Bowa, Schmidt, Luzinski, Boone— wasn't ever going to win a pennant.

At midnight, Owens noted that September had arrived. The month when pennants were won. Time was running out on this team.

Finally, out of cigarettes and sympathetic listeners, Owens pushed the cash that remained on the bar toward the bartender and headed for the elevator. Perhaps a good night's sleep might help. Perhaps he'd feel better in the morning.

He didn't.

◆ ◆ ◆

Something was wrong with the batting cage at Candlestick Park. Workers couldn't get it to open up completely, and batting practice, for both teams, had to be delayed. By the time the Phillies finished hitting and taking infield, there was barely enough time before the game to change into their playing jerseys. They hustled back into the clubhouse.

Owens was waiting for them there.

"Dallas said, 'Pope, we're running late. You wanna do this tomorrow instead?' I told him no. I said, 'I won't need very long to say what I've got to say,'" recalled Owens.

"He said, 'Pope, you're still pissed, aren't you?' And I said, 'God damned right!'"

Then they remembered the call-ups. This was September 1, the day rosters were allowed to expand. The Phillies had brought up pitcher Marty Bystrom, catcher Don McCormack, infielder Luis Aquayo, and outfielder Jay Loviglio from Triple A Oklahoma City. A few others from Double A Reading would be arriving a day later. The Triple A contingent had flown in this morning and, unaware of what was brewing around them, were dressing at their lockers.

"What about the kids, Pope?" Green asked. "You want them in here?"

"Do they have a 'P' on their damn uniforms?" Owens spat. "They're Phillies, too, and they're going to hear what I have to say!"

Owens gathered the players in a corner of the clubhouse. He didn't want anybody hiding in a locker. The call-ups huddled together near a pillar. The general manager's face and bald head were flushed. His hands were trembling. His right leg tapped an unconscious beat on the carpeted floor.

"You guys have been playing for yourselves, fighting among yourselves, complaining for five months," he recalled beginning. "It's going to stop. Dallas has been trying to tell you to straighten out. Now I'm telling you, and Ruly agrees with me 1,000 percent. Stop your pouting and crying. You don't give a damn about winning this thing for yourself. You don't give a damn about winning it for Dallas. Well, then win it for me and Ruly, because we're the ones that put this team together.

"I stuck my neck out for you guys. I kept you together for one more run at it. You've got the talent. But for some reason you don't use it. You worry too damn much about your own little problems. Dallas screamed at you in Pittsburgh, and now you're back doing the same god damned sloppy things."

Now, his anger rising along with his voice, Owens looked at Bowa.

"I bragged him up a little first. I said, 'I've been watching you play since you were a little shit in Sacramento. You're one of the best fielding shortstops ever. But lately you've been letting the ball play you. If I see you one more time short-arm a ball or not take that extra step because you're going after some god damned defensive record, I'm going to pinch your little head off like a god damned grape.'"

Then he turned to Maddox.

"I bragged him up, too. Then I said, 'Hell, anybody can forget their sunglasses and lose a ball in the sun.' But when you do it twice I've got to wonder what the hell's going on with you. I'm god damned sick of your moods and your pouting. All you guys can pout someplace else. I don't want it in this clubhouse anymore."

He challenged Maddox and everyone else to fight.

"You don't like this, come knock on my door. I'm in Room 413. I'm 56 years old, and you might knock me down. But I'll get back up. And as soon as Don Seger (the trainer) patches me up, I'll be back at your door. And I'll keep coming back until you sons of bitches understand that you're a good ballclub."

At one point, Owens looked up. The five new players were in a tight little ball near the pillar, like frightened kittens waiting for their mother to return. The expressions on their faces said, "If this is the big leagues, maybe I should have gone to law school."

This time the reaction was more immediate than after Green's outburst on August 10 in Pittsburgh. Players appeared genuinely moved. They liked and respected Owens. He wouldn't scream unless he had good reason.

"He's more like a father to this team," said Rose. "He developed Bowa, Luzinski, Boone, Christenson, [Randy] Lerch. He traded for some other key guys. He signed me. He means more to this ballclub than Al Rosen means to the Yankees, or Dick Wagner means to the Reds. When he speaks, ballplayers know he didn't go to Harvard or Yale. He speaks a ballplayer's language."

In one sense, Owens's address had a positive impact. The Phillies went out and beat the Giants 6–4. They swept the series, went 23–10 the rest of the way, and won 12 one-run games in the month.

"We got some good things done teamwise," Green said the following day. "I think we're as close a ballclub right now than we have been in a long time."

That was wishful thinking. The pouting and griping wouldn't ever really stop. It was as much a part of the 1980 Phillies as ugly blue road uniforms and bad haircuts. Still, the next time Owens showed up in the clubhouse, on the night of October 4 in Montreal, the mood had lightened considerably.

◆ ◆ ◆

On the wall of Owens's Veterans Stadium office hung a framed 75-cent check. It was the investment that led him into the major leagues.

Owens had played semipro baseball while putting himself through St. Bonaventure College. In 1951, at 27, he graduated. Married, a World War II veteran who had landed on the beaches of France on D-Day, he was set to begin a career as a gym teacher in his hometown of Salamanca, New York.

"A friend called and said he was the new GM at Olean in the Pony League," Owens said. "He wanted to know if I would try out."

He agreed and arrived at the ballpark early one afternoon. A sudden rainstorm canceled his workout. The GM told him to stay for that night's game, that he would leave a ticket. When Owens returned in the evening, he was too embarrassed to ask for the ticket. He bought one for 75 cents.

What took place next sounds like the script for one of those awful 1940s baseball movies. Olean's first baseman broke his jaw in warm-ups. The GM spotted Owens in the stands and told him to get his glove and spikes out of his car. He dressed hurriedly, introduced himself to his teammates, singled, and doubled.

Owens stayed, ended up hitting .407 that year, and was named the league's MVP. After the season, the GM sent him the 75-cent check, reimbursing him for his fortuitous ticket purchase.

By 1955, Owens was back at Olean, managing a Phillies farm club.

◆ ◆ ◆

Owens was a second-year manager in the Phillies organization when, in the winter of 1956, he traveled to Clearwater. The organization used to bring its top 25 prospects to Florida early each February for some up close instruction.

One afternoon, walking past a cage, he heard a booming voice raised in anger. The big, young pitcher on the mound was yelling at someone.

"I stopped because you didn't often hear a voice like that," he recalled. "I just hung around the cage and watched the kid for a while."

Owens liked what he saw. Dallas Green, 21, 6-foot 5-inches, solid as a Louisville Slugger, had just finished his first season at Salt Lake City. An arm injury three years later in Buffalo would transform him from a top prospect to a journeyman, but in 1956 he threw very hard and intimidated hitters—a Don Drysdale clone.

"I liked his makeup right away," said Owens. "He was a very personable guy. Tough. No-nonsense. He was a competitor, and he was the same all the time. He didn't change his personality when he had to talk to the manager or a coach. And he was a lot like me in that if you didn't love the Phillies 110 percent, he didn't want anything to do with you."

The two formed an immediate bond. And on their climbs up through the organization, they passed each other a few more times.

Green remained a top prospect. The Phillies' scouts had found him in Carpenter's backyard, at the University of Delaware, where he played basketball, too. But in 1959, on a cold April day in Buffalo, when Lake Erie was frozen and the wind stung his face, his arm gave out.

He rested it for four months, and when he came back, against Rochester, his wife, Sylvia, could hardly watch.

"They were just belting him," she said. "Run after run. I just sat there and cried. See, I knew what he'd been able to do."

Still, his heart was as big as his vocal cords, and by 1960, Green was a Phillies rookie. That same year Owens had been named the team's new southern California scout.

Green's big-league career stalled under Mauch. The manager had hardly any faith in young players and, when it came to Green, their type-A personalities clashed.

Their worst moment came in late July of 1964. The Phillies were in first place and Mauch was maneuvering like crazy to keep them there. He played Richie Allen and Johnny Callison every day. Chris Short and Jim Bunning were rotation fixtures. And relievers Jack Baldschun or Ed Roebuck usually had the ball late. Beyond that, nothing was certain.

Mauch mixed-and-matched, sometimes using statistics as his guide, sometimes whim. He understood the Phils were not in first place on ability, so every game took on a special significance for him.

On that day, the Cardinals rocked Green for four runs. When Mauch came to get him, he was brutally frank on the mound.

"You're going back to Little Rock (the Phils Triple A club at the time)."

The pitcher was crushed.

"It was really a blow," he said. "My dad was dying of cancer. Two weeks later, he gave it up and died. I still think that's what killed him."

Mauch brought him back in September, but by then the desperate manager had given up on almost all of his pitchers except Bunning and Short.

Green never won more than seven games in the majors. He drifted to the Senators in 1965, the Mets in 1966, and back to the Phillies for eight games in 1967. That last stint came about because Owens saw that the pitcher still needed a few more days in the major leagues to qualify for a pension.

"I really liked him," said Owens. "I thought there would be a place for him in the organization. I knew he and Mauch weren't the best of friends. But Mauch just didn't trust young players. That's how we lost Ferguson Jenkins (in a 1966 trade with the Cubs)."

Curiously, for a journeyman pitcher, Green's otherwise lackluster career included two historic moments.

In a 1963 game with the Mets, Green yielded flaky Jimmy Piersall's 100th home run. Piersall marked the occasion by running around the bases backward.

Then on July 19, 1964, Cincinnati rookie Pete Rose connected for a grand slam off him. It would be the lone grand slam of Rose's long, hit-filled career, a fact he never let Green forget when the two were reunited in 1979.

Bob Carpenter chose Owens to run the Phillies' farm system in 1965. Two years later, when Green's playing days ended, Owens asked if he wanted to join him.

"But first I told him I wanted him to manage in the minor leagues," Owens said. "Dallas wasn't too hot on the idea. I told him he was going to ride buses for 15,000 miles. He wouldn't see much of his family. He'd been in the big leagues, and this wasn't going to be anything like that. He wasn't going to be sitting around a clubhouse having Jim Bunning teach him how to play chess. This would be the hardest thing he ever did."

Green managed at Huron in 1968, where he converted Trillo from catching. He moved on to Pulaski in the Appalachian League and won a pennant. The next year Owens brought him to work with him. When he succeeded Quinn, he named Green to fill his job as farm director.

Scouting and developing suited Green well. Managing often brought out the worst of his volatile nature. Ten years later, with the system turning out All-Star-caliber players, and the big-league team a fixture in the postseason, Green thought he saw his future. He'd do this until Owens retired, probably in the early 1980s, and then move into the general manager's job.

So in August of 1979, when the GM told Green he wanted him to replace Ozark and stay on for 1980, there was an initial reluctance. He'd seen what this group had done to Ozark. But Green was a loyal company man. He agreed.

"How tough could it be?" he thought.

◆ ◆ ◆

Owens took over the Phillies' minor leagues at a most interesting time—ten days before the first major-league draft.

"I had to work like hell to catch up. I went through every scout and looked at every guy he signed," said Owens. "Saw how many made it, how many got hurt, how many washed out. Then I fired eight of them and put two on probation. Hired ten new guys."

Next he turned his attention to facilities. The Carpenters weren't afraid to spend money on players—particularly on the big, hard-throwing pitchers they favored—but they sometimes pinched pennies in other areas.

"What I tried to do was convince Bob (Carpenter) that we needed a minor-league complex in Florida," said Owens. "He kept telling me that we didn't need one, that the way it worked now (with each minor-league club doing its preseason training independently) was working out just fine.

"Finally, I said, 'Mr. Carpenter, which teams beat your ass every year?' He said the Dodgers, the Cardinals, another couple of teams. And I said, 'Well, do you know what every one of those clubs has in common? A minor-league complex.'"

"How much will it cost me?" he asked.

"We can get it done for $200,000," said Owens.

Persuaded, Carpenter agreed to build a first-rate complex in Clearwater. Soon the owner could be found there every morning in February and March, roaming the fields, watching his players more closely than he ever had.

"He told me, 'Paul, I wish I had done this a long time ago.'"

In 1968, just three years after Owens got the job, Topps named the Phillies farm system the best in baseball.

"We started to think," Owens said, "that maybe a World Series wasn't such a crazy dream anymore."

◆ ◆ ◆

The 1980 Phillies began to take shape on the wall of a Los Angeles hotel room.

Owens was staying at the Ambassador Hotel in Los Angeles during the 1965 World Series when he got a call from Eddie Bockman, the Phillies' West Coast scout.

"He said, 'I've got this kid I want you to see. He's a middle infielder from Sacramento. Larry Bowa. Wasn't drafted.'

"Eddie was one of the first guys that liked to take movies of kids he scouted, and he had a bunch of them on Bowa. I told him I was always looking for middle infielders and that he should come up to my hotel room and we'd watch them. He spent half the day riding around L.A. in cabs trying to get all the right equipment. Then when he finally gets to the room, he doesn't have a screen.

"So we looked around and finally we tore the sheet off the bed, grabbed some Scotch tape out of my briefcase and hung it right there on the wall."

Owens saw right away that Bowa had soft hands and above-average speed, but he was only about 150 pounds and it looked like he'd have trouble hitting professional pitching.

"How much will it take to sign him?" Owens asked.

"I can get him for $1,000."

"Hell, I thought you were going to say $10,000. You've spent more than that on cab fares today," said Owens. "Go get him. And give him something extra for shoes and a glove."

Bockman didn't tell his GM much about Bowa's makeup. The kid was as feisty as they came. A borderline head-case, some scouts thought. He apparently came by it naturally. His father, Paul, had been a temperamental minor-league player and manager in the Cardinals organization.

"My father once spiked his own brother in a game," said Bowa. "Gave him 28 stitches in the leg."

Bowa needed to play that way, too. He performed best when he felt he had to prove himself. His high school coach in Sacramento had cut him three times. Scouts derided his offensive skills. Opponents rode him endlessly.

"Don't tell me I can't do something," he said. "That just gets me pissed off."

He eventually played American Legion ball and at Sacramento City College. Bockman spotted him on a semipro team in San Francisco.

"He felt like he had to play there," said Owens. "Apparently all the umpires in Sacramento still remembered his dad, and Paul Bowa was afraid they'd take their revenge on his kid."

Bowa could be a terror on the field. When he was 16, his parents used to watch his games from rightfield so they wouldn't have to hear his frequent expletive-laced explosions.

In the Phillies organization, Frank Lucchesi took an immediate liking to the shortstop, and Bowa made steady progress.

When Lucchesi took over as Philadelphia's manager in 1970—their last year at Connie Mack Stadium—he installed Bowa as his starting shortstop. The rookie had just begun switch-hitting, but there were people in the organization who didn't think it, or anything else, would work.

"When we signed him, it was pretty clear that he had a big-league glove," said Owens. "So I told him that if he could just hit .240, he could play for me for a long time."

For a while it looked like even that modest goal would be a problem. Watching balls ping softly off Bowa's bat at spring training in 1968, the sarcastic Mauch joked that he could *see* him hit but couldn't *hear* him hit. One Philadelphia sportswriter later noted that the diminutive Bowa might even have trouble hitting at Williamsport, implying that he was a Little Leaguer.

Bowa never forgot the last insult. Ten years later, on the night the Phillies won a world championship, he brought it up.

"I thought about the writer who said I swung like a Little Leaguer," he said. "And I said, 'Oh yeah, look at me now.'"

He recovered to hit .250 that rookie season and virtually the same in each of the next two years. In 1972 he led the league in triples with 13 and won the first of his two Gold Gloves. His speed made him ideal for the new artificial surfaces then covering the fields in big, circular, multipurpose stadiums in Philadelphia, Cincinnati, St. Louis, and Pittsburgh.

Even then his temper was making headlines. When, late in the 1972 season, Owens pinch-hit for him, Bowa blew up.

"Tell him I want to be traded," Bowa blared to reporters.

The message relayed, Owens had a scatological reply. "Tell the little asshole to go shit in his hat. He's all right as long as he gets his hits and to hell with the ballclub."

That same year Green mentioned that one of his minor-league prospects, 23-year-old shortstop Craig Robinson, might soon be starting in Philadelphia. Bowa, only 26, stewed.

"It hurt me that our minor-league director didn't think I should be playing," he said. Seven years later, when Green became his manager, Bowa still hadn't forgotten the slight.

He slumped to .211 in Ozark's first season. Bowa had little faith in the manager and chafed on numerous occasions throughout the next seven seasons. But, surrounded by so much talent now, he enjoyed his best seasons—hitting .305 in 1975, .294 in 1977, and being named to five All-Star teams (1974, '75, '76, '78, '79).

When Green arrived in the dugout in 1979, Bowa was wrapping up a disappointing offensive season. Emotionally, the hulking manager and the little shortstop might have been twins. Both were hotheads. Neither could control his mouth. The two sparred often in the clubhouse and in the headlines.

"Dallas is just like me," Bowa said. "He just says stuff."

"Larry is a lot like me," said Green. "He says what's on his mind, then it's over with. He doesn't hold grudges, and neither do I."

A thumb injury limited Bowa offensively in 1979. His average dropped 53 points, to .241. When he got to camp in 1980, he read about shortstop Garry Templeton's new contract (which dwarfed his) and about the possibility of a strike. The longest, most satisfying and maddening season in Bowa's life was ready to roll out of the station—and he wasn't on board.

"It started in the spring of '80," said Green. "Larry was just getting into that contract squabble with Ruly. Then came the strike talk, and he was right in the middle of that (as a player rep). . . . He got off to a slow start, so I jumped on his back. I'm not the most subtle person in the world, so I'm sure I ruffled his feathers. Over the course of the season, we had our differences and we aired them out pretty good."

◆ ◆ ◆

About the same time the Phillies signed Bowa, Owens was getting reports on a young pitcher and third baseman in southern California. He played for the same San Diego high school that had produced Ted Williams, one of Owens's idols.

Bob Boone was the son of Ray Boone, a major-league third baseman from 1948 to 1960 who had been signed as a catcher. Owens knew the elder Boone, and the two had dinner before the draft.

Agents hadn't yet entered the amateur market, and dealing with a father could be tricky business. You had to weigh his feelings as parent before offering an honest assessment. On the other hand, sometimes fathers were susceptible to a major-league letterhead and a little flattery.

"Paul," Boone told him, "my boy's got a scholarship offer to Stanford. You know what a fine school that is. So unless he can really get a bundle, I think I'd prefer he go to college."

"I said I appreciated him telling me that," said Owens, "and I asked him how much was a 'bundle.' He said $25,000 to $30,000, which was a lot of money then. So I told him he probably wouldn't get that much. He went to Stanford, and I told Eddie Bockman to keep a close eye on him. When he was done there, we took him (as their No. 6 pick in 1969). It wasn't long before the opposite of what happened to his father happened to him. We made him a catcher."

In September of 1972, he was in the big leagues. The next year he was Ozark's regular catcher, hitting .261 with 10 homers and 61 RBIs. Boone was smart and confident and even then handled a staff with care and ease.

Except for Carlton.

The idiosyncratic pitcher didn't waver from his philosophies. He expected catchers to conform to his thinking, not the other way around. McCarver recalled one of his first encounters with the left-hander, during spring training in Carlton's rookie year, 1965, when they were St. Louis teammates.

"He comes up after (an outing) and says, 'Hey'—he didn't call me by my name—'Hey, you've got to start calling more breaking balls when we're behind the hitter.'"

McCarver was by then a six-year big-league veteran. "Well, that really blew my mind. I backed him up against the wall and said, 'You son of a bitch. You got a lot of guts telling me that. What credentials do you have?'"

Carlton didn't like the way Boone set his glove in the middle of the plate and then moved it to accept his pitches. He wanted the glove where the pitch was going to end up. That way the umpires weren't fooled, too. And he didn't care for the young catcher's pitch selection.

"He likes to waste pitches when we're ahead in the count," Carlton said that year. "I don't. I like to get it over with. Strike one. Strike two. Strike three."

Boone, as baseball's owners later would find out during negotiations, could be just as stubborn. He wasn't going to change. So the Phillies went out and reacquired McCarver from Boston in 1975 just to catch Carlton, a pairing that stayed in place until 1979.

Though he was only 24, Boone replaced McCarver as the Phils' player rep when the veteran catcher was dealt to Montreal midway through the 1972 season. Each year, it seemed, Players Association business got more complicated and consumed more time. Boone's Stanford psychology degree lent him intellectual heft in the locker room, and players saw him as the obvious choice.

Marvin Miller soon recognized his combination of brains and guts and made Boone his player representative for the National League. Though soft-spoken and reasonable, Boone developed into one of the players' strongest advocates.

He was an All-Star in 1976, 1978, and 1979, and a Gold Glove catcher in the last of those two years. But he tore ligaments in his knee in a home-plate collision with the Mets' Joel Youngblood on September 13, 1979. That off-season he rehabilitated tirelessly—eight hours a day. He was strong when camp opened in 1980, but soon found himself distracted by all the labor talk.

A lifetime .280 hitter, Boone floated around the .200 mark all that year. The Philadelphia fans, some of whom saw him as a focal point for their dissatisfaction with baseball's labor problems, were vicious.

"It probably was tougher on my wife and family than it was on me," Boone said. "It allows you to keep everything in perspective as far as baseball goes. You recognize that, 'Yeah, I can be on top with one swing of the bat, or I can be at the bottom with one swing of the bat.'"

Boone began the season slowly and hit just .229.

"I never got in a groove," he said. "I was lunging at the ball."

Until the pressure-packed last week of the regular season, he never really looked like himself.

◆ ◆ ◆

Luzinski, a beefy, athletic kid, was an outstanding linebacker at Notre Dame High School in Chicago. The University of Notre Dame wanted him, as did Kansas and 38 other schools. He had signed a letter of intent with Kansas before that year's baseball draft.

"In 1968, our Chicago-area scout was sick, and I got another scout to come in from California and take a look at him," said Owens. "He was a catcher then, but it was his bat that excited everyone. I figured we could make a first baseman or outfielder out of him.

"He was the best looking young hitter I ever saw. He had this sweet compact swing, had plenty of power, and he was very intelligent as a hitter. You'd watch him when the count was 0–2 and even as a high-school kid he would take the pitch the other way. That's very rare.

"The draft was out West that year, so I stopped in Chicago on my way out. His dad was his agent. We drafted him No. 1 and signed him for $35,000 and a new Oldsmobile for his father. That's what clinched the deal. His dad was a working-class guy, and he'd always wanted an Oldsmobile."

Green was his first minor-league manager, at Huron, and Owens told him to take a look at Luzinski at first base. He eventually moved to leftfield and was in the big leagues before he was 21.

Luzinski's first full major-league season was Lucchesi's last, 1972. The 6-foot 1-inch, 225 pound outfielder put up decent numbers for a last-place team, hitting .281 with 18 homers and 68 RBIs. His power totals jumped to 29 and 97 in 1973. He injured a knee on June 5 the next year and missed the rest of the season.

In 1975, he began a run of four straight All-Star appearances. He averaged 32 homers and 111 RBIs and batted over .300 three times in those four seasons, as he and Schmidt established themselves as two of the game's best young power hitters.

By mid-June of 1980, Luzinski had 15 home runs and 31 RBIs and was batting over .290. Then he tore up his knee sliding into second on July 5. He underwent surgery and didn't return until the end of August.

By then, Lonnie Smith was a Rookie-of-the-Year candidate, and Luzinski and Green were angrily sniping at each other.

◆ ◆ ◆

Tony Lucadello thought he was hiding. The Phillies scout would come late to Fairview High's baseball games in the mid-1960s. He'd stand way out in rightfield or sometimes underneath the grandstands (he saved all the coins he found there for his goddaughter's college education).

Lucadello covered Ohio, Indiana, and Michigan for the Phillies, and at Fairview High in Dayton, he'd uncovered a young player he loved. The secret to scouting was keeping secrets, Lucadello believed. That explained his clandestine working conditions.

What Lucadello didn't know was that every scout in the Midwest recognized the houndstooth hat he wore and the player he was bird-dogging. When one or more of them would show up at a Fairview game, they wondered why Lucadello was trying to keep Mike Schmidt under a basket.

Schmidt was a young shortstop who looked destined to be a high pick in the 1967 draft. Then he hurt his left knee. The injury scared off most of the scouts, and Schmidt went to Ohio University to study architecture.

While there he worked with a Cincinnati Reds trainer to rehabilitate the knee and when an Ohio U. player left school, Schmidt joined the team. Then he hurt his knee again, the right one this time. That really scared the scouts—except for Lucadello.

"Tony kept telling me, 'This kid is a player. Don't let the knees scare you. Those knees are all right,'" Owens said.

Lucadello was one of the organization's top scouts. He had uncovered Ferguson Jenkins, Larry Hisle, and Grant Jackson. In his 1971 predraft report, the scout described Schmidt as "wiry . . . raw-boned . . . reminds me of (Jim) Fregosi . . . can drive ball . . . quick bat . . . soft hands . . . good range."

Lucadello suggested Schmidt could still be a No. 1 pick, so Owens wanted to have a look for himself. The draft was approaching and Ohio U. had one doubleheader left.

"Tony called me and told me to get out there," said Owens. "The doubleheader was due to start at 10 or 10:30. I got on a plane to Columbus early that morning. Tony met me at the airport, and we drove down to Athens. On the way, it started to rain like hell."

Arriving on campus, Owens begged the baseball coach not to cancel the games. He told him this would be the only opportunity he had to watch Schmidt. The coach said he'd like to play, too, but the field was a muddy mess.

"I suggested he find some gas burners," said Owens. "He did and he had them blowing on that field for an hour or so. The grass blackened. But they played, and Schmidt hits this long, long home run in the first game. All I could think was, 'I've got that god damned Bowa at shortstop. I could move this kid to third, and we'd be set for ten years.'

"I was wrong. It was 15."

Owens selected Roy Thomas, an 18-year-old right-handed pitcher from California, in the first round. He gambled that Schmidt's knees would make him available in the second. He was right, and after some mild negotiations, the Phillies signed him for $32,500.

Schmidt played that first year at Double A Reading. He hit only .211, but by that September he was in Philadelphia. The following season Ozark installed him as his third baseman. Though brilliant at times, he was still a year away. He was an All-Star in 1974, leading the NL with 36 homers and driving in 116 runs. He would hit 30 or more homers in 12 of the next 13 seasons and win a barrelful of individual awards.

But he always seemed marooned on some distant planet. Things looked so easy for Schmidt on the field and so damn difficult off it. He fought himself so hard that he often collapsed when his team needed him most. The vultures in the Veterans Stadium grandstand quickly sensed prey. Here was someone, they believed, who couldn't hit in the clutch.

Schmidt could never learn to answer questions from the media simply and directly. He rambled until he reached some forbidden subject—and then he continued on. Often his words landed him in trouble with fans, who wrongly perceived him as uncaring. Sometimes he infuriated his manager, his teammates, the beat writers.

"Mike had his own way," said Owens. "It seemed like every time he opened his mouth, the wrong thing came out."

Even in his great years, even through much of the wonder-ful stretch run in 1980, Schmidt never appeared to be enjoying himself. He hated the way he whipped himself toward perfec-tion. He longed to be someone he wasn't. He looked at Rose and saw a great player who ignored distractions that would have driven him to a nervous breakdown. Schmidt wanted to be a player who drank beer after games with his teammates and swapped jokes, but his obsessive personality wouldn't allow it.

"I even went to the bathroom at the same time before every game—7:25," he said. "There was always something gnawing at me, something that wouldn't allow me to free myself up to enjoy that whole ride. I don't know how I got so intense about life, so intense that I forgot it should be a lot more enjoyable."

By the late 1970s, he was a favorite target of the city's boobirds. On his way to two straight MVP awards, he became a baseball version of Greta Garbo, wearing big hats and sun-glasses so he could avoid being recognized at McDonald's.

"In Philadelphia I was afraid—not so much afraid, but uncomfortable—to go places," he said. "Restaurants, malls, the kids' functions at schools, airports. I was a recluse."

And like many before and after him, he could not compre-hend Philadelphia's fans. Here he was, on his way to the Hall of Fame, admired by many as the best third baseman of all time, and yet he dreaded home games.

"I had some periods, even during my best years, when I just didn't understand the mentality of the sports fans of Phila-delphia," he said. "I went out there every night not knowing what kind of reaction I was going to get, but pretty sure it was going to be negative."

The blue-collar city took a long time warming up to a player who looked like every game was just another day at the office.

"Obviously, Lenny Dykstra, Pete Rose, Gary Matthews,

those guys gave the appearance that 'Hey, this guy loves the game. This guy will do anything to win. This guy works harder than anybody.' If I knew then what I know now about appearance on the field, I would have dove into more bases, dove after more balls. I dove for a lot of balls, but not one fourth as many as Graig Nettles or Pete Rose or, for that matter, Brooks Robinson.

"We all play the game the way we grew up playing it," Schmidt said. "I played hard. I just didn't get my uniform as dirty."

◆ ◆ ◆

With Bowa and Luzinski in the big leagues, Boone and Schmidt on the way, the Phillies went looking for pitching when the 1971 season ended. That was ironic. Bob Carpenter loved pitchers. He had even tried to move Willie Mays to the mound. The Phillies had signed a ton of them. But, like Green, most of them broke down.

When Owens arrived in Clearwater, the first thing he always did was phone Phillies GM John Quinn. In 1972, that day came on his wedding anniversary. Quinn invited the Owenses to join him and his wife for dinner.

"So we're sitting at the table and our wives are gabbing. Now John Quinn was a very fastidious man. He never liked to discuss baseball around the ladies," said Owens. "But all of a sudden he kind of leaned over to me and whispered, 'I got a call from (Cardinals general manager) Bing Devine.'"

Quinn's manner and the tiny grin on his face made it appear that he had state secrets to share. Owens discreetly asked him what names had been mentioned. Quinn looked around to make sure the women or a waiter weren't listening. He leaned over to his aide again.

"Carlton for Wise."

"Even up?" Owens asked in amazement, his voice rising in excitement.

Quinn put a silencing finger to his lips and nodded affirmatively.

"What do you think?"

"Take it, John!"

"Don't you want to check around?"

"I don't have to, John. I was in New York in 1969 on the night when he struck out 19 Mets. I love Rick. He's probably one of the top five pitchers in our league. But this guy is tall, rangy and he's got such a natural delivery that I don't think he'll ever hurt his arm."

Devine had informed Quinn that morning that Carlton had been holding out for $55,000 and Cardinals owner Augie Busch, the Budweiser baron, was refusing to budge from $50,000. Busch wanted him gone.

"Call me back at 9:30 tonight," Devine had said.

It was all Owens could do to keep from inhaling his fish. He and Quinn raced through the meal and quickly returned to the GM's Fort Harrison Hotel suite. While the wives talked in the living room, they entered the bedroom, closed the door and called Devine.

This time Devine said that as far as he was concerned the deal was done, but he needed to check one final time with St. Louis manager Red Schoendienst. He told Quinn to call him back at 9:15 the following morning.

Anxious torture. That's how Owens recalled that night 28 years later. But the following morning Quinn phoned to tell him he and Devine had made the deal.

"I figured we were on our way then," Owens said.

Carlton was spectacular in 1972, especially given the last-place club that surrounded him. He put together one of the great years in modern pitching history in his first Philadelphia season. Carlton won 27 games, lost just 10, had an ERA of 1.97, threw 30 complete games, and struck out 310 hitters—for a 59-win ballclub.

He was pure power pitcher then. But in 1973, this reclusive man found himself in demand for banquets and ads and interviews. His elbow began to ache. That combined with the distractions to make him a .500 pitcher. From 1973 to 1975, Carlton was 44–47.

"(Then in 1976) he resumed his stature as a power pitcher," said McCarver, "but now he had 12, 13, 14 years of experience to go with it. So he was first a power pitcher, then a pitcher, then a power pitcher with experience."

The grueling sessions with his training guru Gus Hoefling helped him rediscover the power. Then, through the study of Zen and his eventual decision not to talk with the media, he shut out the outside world.

"As far as I'm concerned," he said in a rare interview after the 1980 season, "the press is one of the biggest enemies you have in Philadelphia."

He became a tightly focused martial artist on the mound. Carlton developed a devastating slider and from 1976 through 1979 compiled a 78–41 record, lifting the Phillies to three straight division titles in the first three of those seasons.

◆　◆　◆

The other members of that championship team came in slowly as, year by year, Owens moved to complete the puzzle.

McGraw and Maddox arrived in 1975. Reed in 1976. McBride in 1977. Trillo, Rose, Gross, and Unser in 1979. Christenson, Warren Brusstar, and Ruthven rose through the system.

For Unser and Ruthven, it was a return trip to Philadelphia. Unser had been the Phillies' centerfielder before Owens moved him to the Mets in the trade that brought him McGraw.

Ruthven went to the White Sox in 1975 for Jim Kaat. He moved on to Atlanta where Ted Turner's boorishness aided the Phillies. The Braves owner made a pass at Ruthven's wife at a team cocktail party. Ruthven demanded a trade.

By the midpoint of the 1977 season, the mustachioed, slider-pumping Brusstar's emergence in the bullpen made Gene Garber available. When Owens went looking for starting pitching near the trading deadline, he found out about Turner's indiscretion. Offering the Braves Garber, they jumped at the deal.

Ruthven, a breaking-ball pitcher, had the same problem as a lot of his new Phillies teammates: He could be his own worst enemy. Like Schmidt, Ruthven often was accused of thinking too much, of paralysis by analysis.

The son of a mother with a master's degree in nursing and a civil-engineer father, Ruthven agreed.

"At times I almost wish that I was born a moron so I wouldn't have to think so much," he said.

The McBride trade—he and Steve Waterbury from St. Louis for Dane Iorg, Tom Underwood, and Rick Bosetti—finally settled a longstanding problem in rightfield for the Phillies.

Ozark had played all sorts of journeymen and kids out there—Mike Anderson, Jerry Martin, Jay Johnstone, Ollie Brown, Jose Cardenal, Bobby Tolan. In McBride, he got a player who combined speed, average, defense, and some power.

His line-drive strength was surprising because McBride used one of the smallest bats in the league, a 32-inch model. He did so, he said, because it made him nearly jam-proof.

"With my stance and the way I hit, it's best that I use a short bat," he explained. "As close as I crowd the plate, if I went to a bigger bat, they'd come inside."

By then Ozark and Owens had learned that outfield speed was essential on Astroturf. And while they were stuck with the leaden-legged Luzinski in left, they now had Maddox and

McBride to cover the other ⅞ of the carpeted outfield.

Maddox had grown up in poverty in Los Angeles. An average player in high school, he was drafted in the second round by the San Francisco Giants, who signed the naive 19 year old for $1,000.

When Maddox got to the Giants' Rookie League team in Fresno, he saw that players drafted far lower than him had signed for considerably more money.

"I didn't appreciate that," he said.

Maddox was disillusioned. When the season ended, he and two friends enlisted in the army. The Vietnam War was at its height, and enlistees were being sent overseas right from boot camp.

"It was tough," he said. "For Americans used to the comfort of the United States, it was difficult. It definitely had an impact on my life."

Maddox returned after his tour in Vietnam to care for his ailing father. In the meantime, his father contacted the Giants and explained his son's odyssey. In 1971, Maddox was back at Fresno. By 1972, he was in San Francisco—as Willie Mays's heir apparent.

"There was no way I was going to live up to that comparison," he said.

He hit .268, .319, and .284 in his three years with the Giants.

Owens, knowing Unser's limitations, spotted Maddox early. When the Giants made an inquiry about Willie Montanez early in the 1975 season, the Phillies had their man.

"Everyone talks about being strong up the middle so much that it's a cliche now," said Owens. "But it's really true. Up the middle, we were better than anyone. And Garry Maddox was a big, big part of that. That was one of the reasons we won in 1980."

Chapter 4

Starting to Make Some Noise

Better is the end of a thing than the beginning.

ECCLESIASTES, 7:8

ormally Dallas Green is a neat and tidy man. Except for his mouth, there generally is nothing dirty about him. That's why Phillies players stood there in stunned silence when he dove headfirst into a mud puddle like a 280-pound hog.

It was April 10, the last day of 1980's strike-shrouded spring training. Green and several pitchers were walking off the Clearwater field for a final time when he spotted the standing water. The huge manager got a running start and, hands outstretched, sprawled into the mess.

While the cool Carlton faction ignored him, pitchers Tug McGraw, Randy Lerch, Kevin Saucier, and others soon emulated their manager's filthy fling.

Green's mud-splattered punctuation at the end of training camp was more than a capricious outburst. He had spent much of the spring riding this veteran team like a drill sergeant. Now he needed to try to show them he had another side. He wasn't the bullhorn-voiced bastard they believed him to be. Well, actually he was a bullhorn-voiced bastard, but he was something else, too. He could—literally as it turned out—get down in the dirt with them.

On Opening Day in Philadelphia, Eagles coach Dick Vermeil, whose team shared the stadium with the Phillies, stopped by Green's office to wish him luck in the new season. Green mentioned his dive into the mud, and Vermeil told him he had done the same thing at the Eagles training camp.

That shouldn't have been a surprise. The manager's first spring had a distinct football flavor to it. He, and to some extent Rose, had brought a football mentality to the Phillies.

Green was the vociferous coach, cajoling, belittling, and berating. Rose, the son of a semipro football star, performed with a visible fire, steamrolled catchers, sprinted to first after walks, and snapped his head back toward the umpire as he followed pitches he knew damn well were balls.

Big-league ballplayers, perhaps because the game has little physical contact and few instances when emotion makes a difference, tend to be the least "Rah-Rah" of professional athletes. Baseball has no cheerleaders, no equivalent to the rousing halftime pep talk. If football, hockey, and basketball are hot sports, baseball is decidedly cool.

While the frenetic touchdown celebration had become the measure of NFL chic by 1980, there was nothing cooler in baseball than trotting slowly, dispassionately, around the bases after a home run. Hell, standing still—to admire a long homer—was considered hotdogging in baseball. And the height of player-manager communication was a silent sign flashed by an intermediary, the third-base coach.

Green definitely leaned more toward Walter Camp than Walter Alston. Baseball managers understood that the roller-coaster nature of a 162-game schedule rewarded the even-

tempered. The game moved slowly and so did they. They coun-
seled patience above all else.

Football coaches, on the other hand, were more verbal, forever offering inspirational slogans to their teams, pushing players toward the passionate, physical outbursts the game
required.

"Ozark's 'Let 'em play' approach has been replaced by
Green's 'Make damn sure they play' approach," noted Frank
Dolson, a columnist for the *Philadelphia Inquirer*, in the spring
of 1980.

Green didn't expect his club to turn into the Green Bay
Packers, but he did look for their emotional temperature to rise
a bit in 1980. He even had a punching bag installed in Veterans
Stadium's weight room before the season—a piece of equipment
that must have sagged like a slept-on pillow by 1980's end.

When he talked about character, it didn't mean he
expected the Phillies to celebrate each victory, bemoan every
loss. He just hoped they would look at themselves—and realize
that it wasn't a sin to want badly to win.

"I'm sick of all that macho cool crap," he said.

When the Phillies walked into the clubhouse in February
and saw a big "We Not I" sign, they thought they had landed on
some alien planet. The sign provoked more criticism than
resolve.

"When do the fucking pom-pom girls get here?" shouted
Bowa.

"There were guys who saw that as something better suited
to high school," said John Vukovich.

And when Green began to preach togetherness, it sounded
phony to their ears.

"I think the 'We Not I' concept is fine, but the manager
should be part of the 'We,'" said Schmidt after the season. "I

think there were too many times he used the term 'They' when referring to the players."

Right from the start in Clearwater, with the sign and his candid comments about players to sportswriters, Green made sure he had a battle on his hands. He wasn't going to win it in Florida. It might be July, maybe even August or September, perhaps never before they appreciated his approach.

"This team has told me it wants to stay together to win a world championship," said Green that spring. "To do it, we're going to have to search ourselves, forget the 'I' and think of 'We.' Forget our petty problems. We've got to be able to set those aside and think of the team for a year."

◆　◆　◆

Salary gripes by Bowa and Maddox tested the manager's new theme immediately.

Maddox, who had a .293 lifetime average and had won five consecutive Gold Gloves, was in the final season of a five-year deal that would pay him $375,000. He and agent Jerry Kapstein wanted $3.6 million for four years. That led to guffaws from the front office and immediate trade speculation.

One report had the Dodgers' Don Sutton killing a deal that would have sent the pitcher to Philadelphia for the center-fielder. Most suspected, however, that Owens would rather give up his bourbon than trade an outfielder with Maddox's range.

Rather than take the easy middle ground between owner-ship and players—a strategy that most managers found com-fortable—Green instead pointed out why Maddox didn't deserve that kind of money.

"He's a singles, doubles hitter," said Green. "You can't do that much with him offensively because he doesn't execute. I can't bunt with him. I can't give him a take sign."

And, oh by the way, Green might have added, he'll be my No. 3 hitter.

After a few weeks more of posturing by both sides, Maddox signed a six-year $4.2 million contract that made him the richest centerfielder in baseball, and the second-highest-paid Phillie (after Rose). But he and Green continued to battle all year.

Bowa had two seasons left on a five-year deal that paid him $300,000 annually. That salary ranked him near the middle of NL shortstops. And Garry Templeton, an offensive-focused shortstop, had just signed for a half-million annually. Bowa believed he deserved more and wanted Carpenter to renegotiate.

"I'm not saying I'm worth $600,000," he said, "but some of these guys making more than me . . . it's a fucking joke."

Now Bowa was forcing Green to take sides in his case as well. How were the shortstop and the manager going to get along? Given Bowa's negative reaction to the "We Not I" theme, probably not very well.

"I won't say shit to Green," Bowa vowed. "If he doesn't bug me about little things, we'll be all right."

Complicating their relationship was the fact that Bowa was the club's player rep now that Boone had become the National League's union leader.

Free agency had scuttled the way baseball people viewed the world. The complex issues it created were a long way from being resolved in 1980. There had been work stoppages in 1972 and 1980. Now Marvin Miller had his increasingly powerful union positioned for another strike. The players had set an April 1 deadline, a threat that hung over Clearwater like the clouds that gathered each afternoon out in the Gulf of Mexico.

◆ ◆ ◆

If the Phillies ever did anything right, it was choosing Clearwater, Florida, as their spring-training base in 1947. More than a half-century later, as most other teams shifted around Florida and Arizona like pieces on a Parchesi board, they were still happy there.

A quiet Gulf Coast community of 15,000 after World War II, Clearwater was blessed with ample beaches, sparkling water, and, usually, superb winter weather. It was just far enough away from Tampa and St. Petersburg to give it an isolated, island feel, and close enough to allow some entertainment options.

Like much of the rest of Florida, Clearwater started to boom in the years after the war. Many of the military veterans who had trained in the city or nearby moved there permanently. When their parents came to visit, many decided to retire to the area.

At first, players and management roomed in big old downtown hotels like the Fort Harrison. But eventually, as they grew financially independent and new bridges opened up attractive barrier islands like Clearwater Beach, Indian Rocks Beach, and Sand Key, they began to rent condos and beach homes.

By 1980, it wasn't unusual, on late February afternoons, to find players sunning themselves on those beaches as the sun set spectacularly over the Gulf of Mexico, or relaxing on local golf courses and tennis courts.

Clearwater grew up around the Phillies. Its population—including many Philadelphians who had come to watch spring training, fallen in love with the area, and relocated—neared 90,000 by the time camp opened in February of 1980.

Always among the first to arrive there each February were Owens and Hugh Alexander, the team's all-purpose scout and

Owens's prime confidante. In 1980 the two veteran baseball men drove to Florida in the general manager's new company car. They preferred that to flying. That way they could eat at some of the roadside restaurants they'd discovered over the years and, more importantly, stop at a bar or two at the end of a long day's drive.

The journey gave these two old bird-doggers a chance to gab and sort things out for the coming year.

"The relationship that Hughie and I had was amazing," said Owens. "We were always on the same page. I traveled with the team most of the time so I got to see the National League. I'd focus on two or three guys every game and by year's end I had pretty much seen them all. I trusted Hughie with the American League.

"If we were getting to the point where we needed a player, I'd call Hughie and tell him to get me a lefthanded-hitting outfielder or something," said Owens. "It always seemed like he already knew that's what we'd be wanting, and he always had a few names ready."

When Alexander showed up in Clearwater or Philadelphia, reporters knew a trade was brewing. He was a crusty Oklahoman whose playing days ended abruptly when he lost his left hand in an oil-derrick accident in 1967.

"I used to say, 'Hughie, you're my right-hand man,'" recalled Owens. "And he'd say, 'Hell, I'd better be. I ain't got a left one.'"

Both had spent considerable time talking with Green that winter so they knew how he felt. Like him, they agreed the club's veteran nucleus ought to be given one final chance. They believed injuries were more responsible than anything else for 1979's disappointment.

The fact that some of the national publications were picking the 1980 Phillies to finish low in the NL East—*Sports Illustrated* had them fourth—didn't concern them at all. Sure, Montreal was improving rapidly, and the Pirates were the defending world champions, but Owens and Alexander knew a healthy Phillies team was at least as good.

Schmidt had become one of baseball's best players. Luzinski was in better shape. Boone was an All Star who had such a good head on his shoulders that he'd be a huge help to the young pitchers they planned on carrying. Maddox and Bowa wanted new contracts, so they'd be primed to go. Rose was Rose. Trillo and McBride were better than a lot of people knew.

Defensively, their infield was the best in baseball, and Maddox and Boone were coming off Gold Glove seasons. Gross and Unser were popular bench players and superb pinch hitters. Nothing needed to be said about Carlton. If Christenson and Ruthven were healthy, they'd be fine. McGraw was a pro. And while Reed was a pain in the ass, he could still help.

"How 'bout them other sumbitches?" Alexander asked Owens.

That's where the revolution would occur. Guys like Rawley Eastwick, Doug Bird, Mike Anderson, Bud Harrelson—comfortable veterans who sometimes acted as if the clubhouse card games took precedence over the baseball games—drove them crazy.

"I got tired of the same old smug looks I saw on the bench," Green told Owens. "Cripes, last September we'd be in a tough ballgame and I'd look down there and it was like ten penguins."

A lot of those penguins, Owens now told Alexander, were going to be iced. He and Green had put a lot of effort into the farm system, and some of their kids—catcher Keith Moreland, outfielders Lonnie Smith and George Vukovich, pitchers like

Bob Walk, Jim Wright, and Scott Munninghoff—were ready.

Besides, this team needed to see the youngsters' passion for the game. You could only talk about wines and God and investments for so long. At some point, baseball players needed to talk and think about *baseball*.

"I knew in my heart that the Dodgers didn't belong on the same field with us in '77 and '78," said Owens. "We just lacked that intangible something a great team needs to have."

They thought they got it in 1979 with Rose. But a remarkable run of injuries never allowed them to find out. In fact, things were headed backward by the end of August when Owens fired Ozark and brought in an attitude-adjuster in Green.

By the time they pulled into Clearwater, Owens and Alexander were convinced that if there were no strike, the 1980 Phillies could win the division. And once they got into the playoffs, who knew what might happen? The Phillies themselves certainly had experienced enough crazy postseason bounces to give hope to any club that got there.

Not far outside of Clearwater, the weather had warmed to the point where Owens reached for the air-conditioning. He couldn't figure out how it worked. Neither could Alexander. When they reached the Fort Harrison Hotel, the two of them took a look.

"Neither of us is too hot with mechanics, so we figured we'd take it to a garage and have them look at it," said Owens.

Then he and Alexander went off to talk with some of the scouts and coaches who also had arrived early. When Owens got back to the hotel, there was a message. The shop had called about his car.

"Tell Mr. Owens," the message said, "that his car doesn't have air-conditioning."

◆ ◆ ◆

Aside from some salary talk and a plea from Green to the beat writers not to focus on Brusstar's rehabilitation efforts, the first days of camp passed uneventfully. There was the typical optimism spiced by a little trade talk.

The names of McBride, Maddox, and Smith surfaced occasionally. One rumor had Lerch and Moreland going to Cincinnati for Ken Griffey. And Owens made no secret that he'd love a veteran reliever, maybe Sparky Lyle from the Texas Rangers or Stan Bahnsen from the Expos.

"I had a lot of people calling me about this guy or the other," said Owens, "but I just said, 'No, I think we're going to see what this team can do with Dallas for a full season.'"

Green got high marks for his organizational skills. Schedules were adhered to, fundamentals were stressed early and often, no one stood by aimlessly, and the work was demanding but so neatly compressed that players still had time for golf and tennis in the late afternoons.

Even the cynical sportswriters were impressed. "(This camp is) professional, efficient, intelligently planned, impartial, and executed without flab and dead spots," wrote Conlin.

By comparison, Ozark's last springs had been marked by a laissez-faire disorder. He permitted the players to set their own agendas. That often included more activity off the field than on it.

"Danny gave the big-league ballplayers more credit than he should have," said Luzinski. "(Letting them do) things on their own to get ready. Dallas is saying, 'I want you guys to do it. I know you'll do it, but it's going to be organized and supervised.'"

Luzinski arrived at camp in great shape, having dropped 15 pounds during a winter when iced tea and lite beer became his beverages of choice. His teammates all looked fit as well, and Green seemed pleased.

"There's a lot of dedication and determination to get this team back where it belongs," he said. "Everybody I've looked at has a flat belly and clear eyes."

Schmidt had stepped aside as captain, a position for which he could not possibly have been more ill suited. Ozark had given him the title without consulting the rest of the team and the third baseman wore it like a Scarlet Letter.

"We had Pete Rose who exemplified what a captain ought to be," said Schmidt, lobbying for a replacement. "I didn't have the personality for it."

Green never did name one.

"What the hell is a captain gonna do besides walk the lineup out to home plate every day?" he asked.

The manager's first real test, at least in the eyes of the media, came when the pitchers arrived. Green stressed conditioning. Old school, he wanted his staff to run until their eyes bugged out. That flew in the face of Carlton's philosophy. The big left-hander believed running was worthless—and who could argue with him?

He worked harder than anyone on the team, even had his fitness guru, Gus Hoefling, appointed the Phillies' strength and conditioning coach. But there was no way he was going to run. And he didn't.

Green chose not to make it an issue.

"Lefty already works harder than anyone else," he said. "When I said the pitchers needed to run, I wasn't referring to him. His conditioning program seems to be working just fine. I did about half the workout Lefty does with Gus at the Vet a few times this winter and it damn near killed me. He doesn't have to run."

◆ ◆ ◆

More and more, talk of the strike dominated camp.

"Nobody's got their mind on the game of baseball now," Green said, "other than the bullshit part of it."

The Phillies never really hit their stride in exhibition games. On April 1, they lost to Texas at Pompano Beach, their fifth straight defeat. As they departed a bus in Cocoa Beach the following day, Green got word from Owens on the Players Association meeting in Dallas. The executive board had voted to delay a strike deadline until May 22, but the players would not finish the exhibition schedule.

"The decision," said Miller, "came after 20 weeks of fruitless negotiations."

The owners had decided to keep open their camps for players who wanted to work out—though adding ominously that anyone not in shape on Opening Day wouldn't play.

Green suggested the team stay in Cocoa Beach. The Phillies would hole up in the Holiday Inn there until events sorted themselves out. It turned out to be superb strategy. While other teams disassembled and scattered, the Phillies held together.

Two days later, the Phillies voted to stay in Clearwater and train together with Green. Except for the fact that they had no one to play but themselves, it was business as usual.

"I don't think anyone will have trouble getting ready physically," predicted Bowa. "It's the mental part that will be difficult."

There were a few obvious differences from normal springs, though. Carpenter ordered all the equipment locked up, perhaps thinking that would discourage players from deserting the camp and working out on their own (though men earning half-a-million dollars a year probably could have afforded a few bats and balls). And there was no housing or meal money.

Some of the Phillies fringe players worried immediately about finances.

"I've got a $1,600-a-month place on the beach," said Bird. "There's no way I can pay for that if I'm not getting expense money."

Two days before the Players Association meeting in Dallas, the Phillies had taken an informal strike vote. Seventy percent of them had voted to walk out immediately. Clearly, their heads were elsewhere.

"We were semi-going through the motions," said Green. "I shouldn't even say semi."

Since federal mediator Ken Moffett had threatened the owners with $500,000 fines if they publicly discussed the labor situation, the rhetoric was kept to a minimum.

Carpenter said the team would be responsible for getting the players from Cocoa Beach to Clearwater. Indicative of the path baseball was on, the players returned on one bus, the coaches, trainers, and equipment men on another.

The relationship between Carpenter and his team was unique. He lived on a rolling estate in northern Delaware— "Ruly's plantation" is how Owens referred to it. He attended private schools, and his blue blood practically showed through his polo shirts. But his father had insisted that Ruly get to know the organization from the bottom up. Working in the farm system, he had developed close ties with Owens, Green, and several of the team's key players.

His business was baseball. The players recognized that. He talked strategy with them, played cards with them. This wasn't Augie Busch, a wealthy dilettante who still ran his beer empire.

"We've got a different type of owner," said Bowa.

Someone asked Carpenter if he thought beginning the season without a signed Basic Agreement would distract his players.

"We were having a hell of a year in '76 before that (agreement) was signed," he said. "After it was signed, we almost blew a 14- or 15-game lead."

"The strike can be disruptive if we let it," said Green. "It will test the character of our team again."

On April 3, Espinosa went on the disabled list with a bad shoulder. Brusstar returned to Oklahoma City to see Dr. William Granna about his ailing shoulder. Green revealed that Munninghoff, a right-handed rookie pitcher, would be going north as one of a ten-man Phillies staff.

That staff still included Christenson, who was beginning to throw well again after getting hit on the knee by a line drive off the bat of Detroit's Jason Thompson earlier in the spring. Christenson, 26, had been banged up for much of 1979, finishing 5–10 in 19 games with a 4.50 ERA.

"I was just never in good shape last year," he said.

The right-hander had a bone spur removed from his collarbone in the off-season and nearly was traded at the winter meetings.

The following day, the ax that everyone sensed was looming over camp finally fell. Eastwick and Bird were cut loose even though the Phils still owed them money on long-term deals. Anderson, once the organization's top prospect, was released, as was Harrelson.

"We wanted to go with the young kids," said Green.

Moreland would be the backup catcher. Smith would see plenty of time in the outfield, and his speed made him an invaluable pinch hitter and pinch runner. With Harrelson being dropped, John Vukovich, in his 15th year of professional ball, would finally start a season in the big leagues. George Vukovich, no relation, would make it, too, now that Anderson was gone.

Some veterans saw the sudden turnover as a selfish move by Green. Before he became manager, Green had pushed Ozark each year to take some of his kids north. Ozark, like a lot of managers, felt more comfortable with veterans.

As soon as Green got the job, there were predictions he soon would stock the roster with rookies. And that's exactly what happened, giving Green another strike against him in the locker room.

"Dammit," Green said in *The Team That Wouldn't Die*, "we spend $3 million a year on player development. How do I justify $3 million to my owner if we don't play the kids we develop? Just because we have long-term contracts doesn't mean they have to play out those long-term contracts in Philadelphia. Sometimes you add by subtracting."

Smith, Moreland, and the others, Green insisted, could play and contribute. But he also realized that they—and maybe especially the vociferous John Vukovich—could perform an even more valuable function. They could add some passion, some character.

"Dallas would use the younger guys to sometimes motivate the older players," said Smith.

Throughout the season to come, the manager would point frequently to his youngsters and Vukovich when he wanted to emphasize an attribute he thought the veterans lacked. They became a counterpoint to the team's raging coolness. Whenever a veteran got complacent, he'd stick a kid in there.

"There's no question in my mind that if we had gone with the same people we had in '79, we would not be champions," said Green. "The kids brought the freshness.

"We had to get some juice. We couldn't count on Tug McGraw slapping his leg and Pete Rose sliding on his belly to do it. That was about the only emotion this team had. Every now and then Larry Bowa got it going pretty good, but to some degree Bowa was part of that old clan, the group that had become very staid in its ways."

First, Green had to convince Owens that the rookies could improve the 1980 Phillies.

"I'd always thought that the most important guys on your ballclub were 8 through 15 among your regular players," said Owens. "That's why that '77 team was so good. We had guys like Ollie Brown, Davey Johnson, and Jay Johnstone who didn't just pinch-hit but were capable of playing a couple times a week.

"So I told Dallas, 'I know you think those kids can play, but I want you to make sure they do. I don't want them sitting around the dugout like ornaments. I'd rather see them get another year's experience under their belts in the minor leagues than have that happen.'"

◆ ◆ ◆

On April 5, Green put the Phillies through a four-hour simulated game. Its purpose was to get his pitchers some live work. Ruthven and Carlton threw 100 pitches each. The marathon almost killed some of his regulars. All but Trillo and Luzinski among the regulars were 30 or older—and they were 29.

"This wasn't a punishment thing," explained Green. "We just had to stretch the pitchers out."

"That's the first time I ever got five hits and had a bad game," said Bowa. "I was 5 for 26."

A few days later Green revealed his starting lineup for the April 11 season opener in Philadelphia. Rose would lead off, followed by McBride, Maddox, Schmidt, Luzinski, Boone, Bowa, and Trillo.

That was a surprise to Bowa who, still trying to work out his contract demands, had spent the spring reluctantly learning to accept hitting out of the No. 8 hole after batting second for much of the last several seasons.

"He didn't hit me seven all spring," said Bowa. "He didn't hit me two. He hit me eight all spring. And now it's going to get changed?"

Now things were really getting rolling.

"With him hitting seventh," said Green in response, "we can use him to steal more bases."

The lineup was healthy and formidable. The rotation, beyond Carlton, was a different story. Ruthven's spring ERA was 7.88. Lerch's was 7.36. Christenson had pitched just $5\frac{2}{3}$ innings. Espinosa was on the DL.

"The big question mark we had coming out of that camp," said Schmidt, "was our starting pitching. We knew we were going to score some runs. We knew we could catch the ball with anyone. We had pretty good team speed, especially when Lonnie played. But heading north, we didn't know what was going to happen to the rotation beyond Lefty and Rufus (Ruthven)."

On the day before they broke camp, Maddox reduced his demand, insisting he would split the difference if the Phillies increased their offer a little. That same day Bowa and Carpenter, back in Delaware, spoke for two hours on the phone. The shortstop still wanted an extra $300,000 added to his contract over the next three years.

The Phillies returned to Philadelphia on the night of April 9. The following night, in a gesture toward fans tired of hearing about a possible strike, they opened the Vet for a public work-out. Four thousand fans showed up.

"Looks like opening night in Atlanta," said Rose.

Chapter 5

Watching a Strike Go By

We had the label of choke artists.

LARRY BOWA

I f anyone thought the mud dive meant Green had backed off now that the regular season was starting, their minds were changed when they got back home.

Several hours before the season opener at Veterans Stadium, in a nearly deserted Phillies locker room, assistant clubhouse manager Pete Cera distributed sheets of paper. Cera was a small and quiet man, nearly invisible at times amid the clubhouse commotion. He made his daily rounds undisturbed, so no one noticed as he deposited the papers on the red chairs that sat in front of each locker.

This was no itinerary for the next road trip, nor an invitation to the opening of a car dealership in South Jersey. Cera was delivering Dallas Green's new Phillies commandments. The Danny Ozark Era was officially over.

Green's rules mandated a dress code ("No jeans unless they're designer jeans"). They prohibited drinking on team flights without the manager's permission. They established a 1 A.M. curfew after day games, 2 A.M. following night games.

Players could not leave the clubhouse until the game finished. Card games were banned as soon as the pitchers began hitting at home, or when the bus arrived at the ballpark on the road.

"Any players acting unprofessionally, or embarrassing me or the club," read the broadest of the commandments, "will be fined at my discretion."

For Green, what his guidelines were saying was "Honor thy organization and thyself." The players read it differently. To them the unnecessary rules stated: "You haveth no hammer. It sitteth in the right hand of Green."

Some players shook their heads in disgust. Just one more example of Green treating them like high schoolers. Bowa scoffed. Someone brought the list to Carlton, scheduled to start that night. He refused even to examine it. He didn't read the newspapers—he called them "poison"—and he sure as hell wasn't going to read this.

The Phillies had built the pitcher a little mood room off the clubhouse where he could be alone with his eccentricities. It had blue carpeting, blue walls, and a tape deck on which he could listen to the sound of crashing waves as, on days like this, he prepared himself mentally for a start.

"We've proven in the past we can win," said Green when asked to justify the rules. "We've also proven that we haven't won the whole ball of wax. The only indication I can come up with is our total approach over 162 games, which comes down to the character of the team. Character can carry you over the bumps, the peaks and valleys that are part of this game."

The team's fans were somewhere between a peak and a valley when the 1980 season opened. They had arisen from their historic torpor when Veterans Stadium opened. Ever since the Phillies began to exhibit some promise in 1974, there had been a steady incline to their hopes, passions, and numbers.

Attendance built from 1.4 million in 1973 to a franchise-record 2.7 million in 1979. But the club's consistent play-off failures disappointed Philadelphians, and the dismal, injury-plagued 1979 season quelled their expectations. Even with Rose, the thinking went, this team might not have what it took to win a World Series.

The preseason publications suggested the same thing. And they raised an issue that Philadelphians had been discussing for years: These Phillies, for all their great physical talents, might not have the guts, the heart, of a champion. Whether that was true or not, it certainly looked that way. There were times when the Phillies performed like swaggering robots. All strut and no stomach.

"We had the label of choke artists," said Bowa. "That's the way fans felt about us. You could argue with them all you wanted but until 1980 we hadn't done anything to convince them they were wrong."

The reality was more complex. The Phillies had a heart. But faced with the quick, stinging rebukes their fans were famous for, they chose not to wear it on their sleeves. Philadelphia fans loved to see hearts on display. The problem was, if you slipped up, it became a big bulls-eye.

Maddox, Schmidt, Boone, and Luzinski had all been targets. They retreated emotionally, becoming among the least demonstrative athletes imaginable. And when the team lost, as it did in 1979, that looked a lot like indifference.

"It wasn't a big shock that guys acted that way," said Bowa. "If Schmitty struck out and the fans were getting all over him, he wasn't going to hang his head and slump back to the dugout or give the finger to the crowd. He was going to try to walk professionally off the field. People perceived that as not caring."

It wasn't easy trying to walk the tightrope that Phillies fans and the city's sportswriters demanded. They not only wanted wins, they wanted wins with hustle and heart. Some players thrived in that atmosphere, others retreated.

"If you were a Philly kind of guy, someone who always had dirt on their uniforms like Pete (Rose)," said Schmidt, "those fans were the best in baseball. But if they saw something that suggested you didn't care, they'd carve you up."

Green knew the mental makeup of his players. They were never going to be fire-breathers on the field. But he still felt that if they dared step outside the comfort zone they had constructed for themselves, they could perform more effectively, with more fire.

Certainly, they had become quite comfortable. That was why Green smashed their traditions with his new rules. That was why he jettisoned those veterans in the spring and added all those rookies.

"If all you're gonna be is comfortable just to suit your own personality instead of thinking about the team, we're not gonna get a lot accomplished in 1980," Green told them.

Despite these concerns, Philadelphians had not abandoned their baseball team. The 18,000 season tickets sold that year ranked the Phillies second in the NL, behind only the Dodgers. Some 4,000 showed up on the night before the opener for a public workout. And despite Bill Giles's dire crowd predictions, 48,460 fans came out on a Friday night to watch Carlton and the Phillies open their season with a 6–3 victory over the Expos, a team expected to challenge for the division title.

That meant, said Giles, about 18,000 tickets had been sold in the days before the opener, a surge he attributed more to the pleasant weather than optimism for the coming season.

The Phillies' 1980 season began with a good omen. Kiteman, a stuntman with a hang glider, had successfully soared from the centerfield stands to a spot near the mound. Several of his predecessors had failed to make it that far at previous home openers. The tricky winds that swirled around the circular ballpark sent them tumbling off their ramp into hard plastic seats or crashing to the turf.

Thus, in Philadelphia, baseball seasons often began *and* ended with notable collapses.

◆ ◆ ◆

When the game started, the relatively svelte Luzinski belted a three-run homer in his initial at bat, on a 2–2 pitch from Steve Rogers in the first inning. It was the best of signs for Green and the fans. With a healthy Luzinski, the lineup went from formidable to frightening.

Circling the bases, Luzinski uncharacteristically pumped a fist in the air. It seemed to be a message to the crowd and to Green, who liked to make him one of his whipping boys. The fans, who had turned on Luzinski in recent seasons and never let him forget that dropped fly ball on Black Friday, summoned him out of the dugout for a curtain call.

"I had a lot of emotion in me, and it had to come out," he said, attempting to explain his emotional gesture. "I really can't tell you what was going through my mind as I ran around the bases."

For Luzinski, 1979 had been the worst season of his life. He was hurt and overweight. His diminished numbers, 18 homers and a .252 average, suggested to many that at 28 he was heading downhill.

"I remember telling Bull this when he was a kid of 21 or 22," said Owens. "I told him that unless he took care of himself he was going to be out of the National League by the time he was 30. He kind of laughed it off. But Bull had a tendency to be lazy about his weight. He used to get heavy in his chest, and I told him that a hitter can't swing the bat as well and a pitcher can't throw as well when he's heavy up there."

With Smith ready, there had been plenty of trade rumors involving Luzinski the previous year. That winter, Carpenter met with him at the player's South Jersey home. He suggested he lose weight and try glasses instead of contacts. He told the outfielder that if the right deal came along, yes, he could be traded, but, no, they weren't actively pursuing a deal.

"It gave me peace of mind," said Luzinski. "And I decided that I was tired of hearing about the weight."

He dropped pounds, going from 238 to 215, and reconditioned himself.

"I think they can see that Bull has put in a lot of hard work during the off-season," said Green of the fans' reaction, "and they appreciate that here."

Meanwhile, Carlton's slider baffled the young Expos.

"The thing comes at you hard as a fastball, and you feel like you've got to swing," said third baseman Larry Parrish, "then at the last second it breaks down about a foot, and you've got no shot at it. It's unbelievable."

The following night, Ruthven beat Montreal as Maddox homered and doubled.

April 15 was an off day, and the Delaware Chapter of the Multiple Sclerosis Society had scheduled a charity roast of Green. One of the night's more humorous, and telling, comments—and one Green was sure to hear if things went badly this season—came from Dolson:

"Only an organization that hasn't won a pennant in 30 years," the *Inquirer* columnist said, "would hire a former pitcher with a 20–22 record to instill a winning attitude."

◆ ◆ ◆

When April ended, the Phillies were 6–9. They had plenty of excuses. Rose wasn't hitting yet, and aside from Carlton, the starting pitching hadn't come around. Christenson and Espinosa still weren't healthy. Ruthven was slow bouncing back from off-season elbow surgery. Lerch, because he was wildly inconsistent and so laid back that his demeanor often suggested laziness, had become one of Green's favorite whipping boys. The young pitcher's head was spinning so fast from all of his manager's public criticisms that he couldn't get anyone out.

"We've got to quit using alibis when we don't do it," said Green. "If we start that bullshit, we won't be the baseball team we think we can be."

They got a boost on May 2 when Ruthven beat the Dodgers 9–5, the first time the right-hander had looked like himself this season. His velocity had improved, and there was snap again on the breaking balls he relied on to put hitters away. Nine days later he would beat the Reds at Cincinnati.

"It's a place to start," said Ruthven.

That victory over the Dodgers also marked the Veterans Stadium return of Ozark, now a third-base coach for Tommy Lasorda. Booed loudly throughout the game, he had been his usual misspeaking self during a radio interview.

"My contract with the Dodgers," Ozark bragged, "says I'm welcome to leave at any time."

Not only did the Phillies start slowly, but the looming May 22 strike deadline depressed them. Players made alternate plans.

Luzinski said he would do public relations work for a South Jersey meat company, "going to meat shows and that kind of stuff." Schmidt had an offer from American Motors. Bowa and Rose planned to head back to Clearwater and work out on their own.

For Americans, a baseball strike would have been just one more indignity to endure in 1980. Inflation was staggering. Mortgage rates were so high no one could buy or sell a home. The auto industry, which continued to turn out big, breakdown-prone gas-guzzlers, was getting slapped silly by the Japanese. The humiliating Iranian hostage crisis remained unresolved. Mount St. Helens had recently erupted. And now a baseball strike?

"It's like America is falling apart," a Phillies usherette told a reporter the day before the deadline.

Four years after the end of the reserve clause, a backlash was building among baseball fans. As salaries rose to unrecognizable levels, resentment built among Americans who suddenly were economically challenged. They were getting laid off. They couldn't afford to fill their car with gas or buy a house. And ballplayers, guys making several hundred thousand dollars a year for playing a kid's game, were going to go on strike?

"My dad was a union guy," said Bowa. "He used to get up at 6 in the morning and get home at 5 every day. And even he was against us. He said, 'What are you guys doing? You're in the major leagues. You make good money. Don't talk about strikes.' I figured if my own father feels that way, how angry must the average fan be?"

Yet, it was just as hard to sympathize with the owners. First of all, they were the ones setting the salary structure. Houston's John J. McMullen had just lowered his counterparts' jaws by six inches when he made free-agent Nolan Ryan the first $1 million a year player.

For all his velocity and his handful of no-hitters, Ryan was basically a .500 pitcher. He had gone 16–14 in his last year at Anaheim, prompting Angels GM Buzzie Bavasi to say he'd have to sign a pair of 8–7 pitchers to replace him.

More significantly, baseball only recently had emerged from the economic slavery of the reserve clause, something even John Birch would have had difficulty defending. Now, just four years into a limited free agency, the owners were demanding a system of compensation that would have rendered it meaningless.

"Some teams are going to go broke," predicted Minnesota owner Calvin Griffith, repeating a lament as old as the game itself. "It's bound to happen."

The union was solidly opposed to retreat. Miller had built a remarkable solidarity among the ballplayers in a short time and everyone—save the owners—recognized that.

"Don't the owners realize that there will be a whole generation of sons of major-league ballplayers who have the middle name Marvin?" asked Yankees pitcher Rudy May.

"I keep hearing that the owners think we're bluffing," said Boone. "If that's what they truly believe, then there is going to be a strike. All the owners are telling us is that they want us to play baseball with a 1976 agreement while they reap 1980 profits."

There was something else to consider in baseball that spring. Guys like Green were always talking about how important chemistry was, how essential it was that teams stay together. A strike could split a ballclub open like an axed watermelon. And what union dissenter would want to face a player rep with a hardball in his hand?

"Anybody who does that (breaks ranks)," said Kansas City's George Brett, "is going to spend the rest of his career in the dirt, ducking pitches thrown at his head."

Negotiations moved on with little progress reported. Finally, late on May 22, word came out of Room 1706 of the Doral Inn in New York City that a settlement had been reached. The new deal made a few small adjustments to the Basic Agreement and saved the 1980 season.

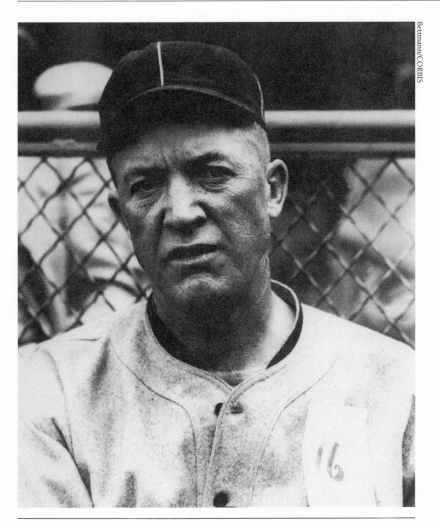

Bettmann/CORBIS

Phillies pitching great Grover Cleveland
Alexander was signed in 1911.

Bettmann/CORBIS

Manager Gene Mauch (right, with Danny Murtaugh) was the manager of the infamous 1964 Phillies, a team that squandered a 6½-game lead in the last two weeks of the season.

Bob Carpenter, center, (seen here with Philadelphia mayor Joseph Clark, left, and Philadelphia A's president Connie Mack, right) owned the team from 1943 to 1972, when he handed the Phillies over to his son, Ruly.

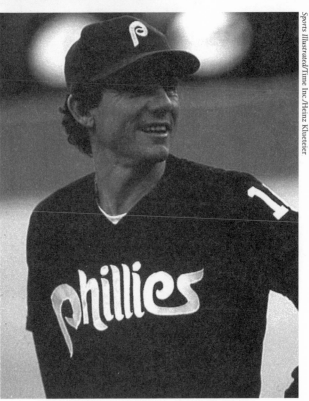

Larry Bowa came up through the Phillies' system with a chip on his shoulder and all the right moves at shortstop.

Mike Schmidt was in his prime when the Phillies
made their World Series run in 1980.

Hurler Steve Carlton lifted the Phillies to three
straight division titles and, finally, a World Series.

General manager Paul Owens got Manny Trillo from the Cubs to give the Phillies more firepower.

Ruly Carpenter was reluctant to acquire Pete Rose, but the former Reds' hit machine was the leader the Phillies needed to win.

Sports Illustrated/Time Inc.

Dallas Green's theatrics got him ejected during a
critical game against the division-leading
Montreal Expos.

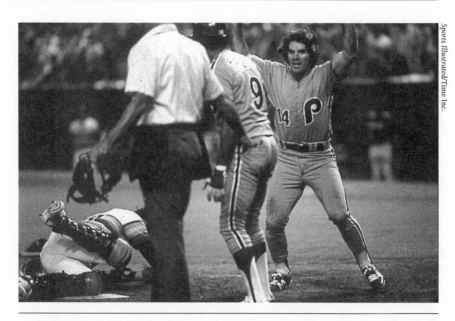

After Rose's hard slide into Astros catcher Bruce Bochy in Game 4,
the Phillies came out of their two-game funk and roared back
into the National League Championship Series.

Green's "We Not I" philosophy wasn't popular in the clubhouse,
but it worked.

Tug McGraw leaps into the air after closing out a game
during the NLCS.

Pete Rose congratulates Bake McBride on his three-run
homer in Game 1.

George Brett, here diving into the photographers' well to make a catch, homered to help the Royals win Game 3.

Phillies Catcher Bob Boone pumps his fist after McGraw fans Jose Cardenal with bases loaded in the bottom of the ninth to end Game 5.

Boone bobbles Frank White's pop-up . . . just before Rose's lightning-quick catch sets the Phillies up for the World Series title.

The team exults in winning Game 5 of the championship series.

Pete Rose with the trophy.

At the celebratory parade, Tug McGraw holds up the front page of the *Philadelphia Daily News.*

The minimum salary was raised from $21,000 to $30,000. The pension plan was improved. But the big issue, free agency, remained unsettled. It was handed over to a four-man committee of players and owners for further study. One of the committee's members would be Boone.

◆ ◆ ◆

A few days later, with a Memorial Day crowd of 45,394 watching at the Vet, the relieved Phillies finally displayed some togetherness.

Having been each other's chief rival since 1974, the Phillies and Pirates shared no great warmth. Because of that, Pennsylvania's teams seemed to relish playing against each other. There had been numerous beanball incidents over the years including the 1977 fight when Schmidt, who had 25 homers in 77 games, broke his right ring finger after charging Bruce Kison in Pittsburgh.

"That team really enjoyed playing against the Pirates," said Rose. "And they were our toughest competition. That showed me something about their character. When we played the Pirates, you should have heard the jibber-jabber."

Now, in their initial 1980 meeting, things got started in the first inning when Pirates starter Bert Blyleven buzzed Schmidt.

"We're still world champions," the pitch suggested. "And we're not going down without a fight." Since his cool act often infuriated opponents, Schmidt got knocked down occasionally. He rarely reacted. But when, with the Pirates leading 5–1 in the third, Blyleven sent the Phillies star spinning to the dirt with another high-and-tight fastball, the normally placid Schmidt pointed a menacing finger at the pitcher and moved toward the mound. Both benches cleared.

Later, reliever Kevin Saucier hit Willie Stargell and then Blyleven, the second incident touching off a major brawl. In that chaotic sixth-inning scuffle, Bowa suffered a cut lip (which for him, teammates joked, was a disabling injury), and Phils pitching coach Herm Starrette was ejected after slugging it out with Lee Lacy. Pittsburgh's Phil Garner and Tim Foli came out of it with bruised faces.

Charged up by the fight and the big crowd, the Phillies rallied to win 7–6 on ninth-inning doubles by Schmidt and Boone and singles by Luzinski and Bowa. The victory moved them atop the NL East by .004 percentage points, the first time they had been there since the season's second game.

"We know that they're the team to beat and they know that we're the team to beat," explained Rose, perhaps a bit too literally given the night's events. "You're going to see a lot of hard baseball played between these two teams. Not too bad for the first of 18 games, huh?"

Green appreciated the way his players had battled side-by-side. It had been the manager's experience that brawls sometimes helped unite a ballclub. Even the bullpen pitchers and coach Mike Ryan, a New Englander who loved a good slugfest as much as a nicely steamed lobster, had come charging into the fray.

So the manager was puzzled and angry when the Phillies dropped six of their next eight games. A week later in Pittsburgh, when McGraw gave up a game-winning, ninth-inning hit to Ed Ott, they had fallen four games behind the Pirates.

The offense had cooled considerably, and only Carlton's brilliant first half was keeping them in the race. The Phillies ace won his tenth game on June 4, beating Pittsburgh 4–3. He was 10–2. Without him, the Phillies were 14–19.

"That first half of Lefty's season was the most remarkable thing I've ever seen in baseball," said Boone, who resumed catching the Phillies ace in May of 1979. "He was in such total command. He didn't make a single mistake in all that time.

Two, three months without missing a pitch. It was phenomenal. Just phenomenal."

In his next start, five days later against the Giants at home, Carlton retired the first 13 hitters he faced. But rain interrupted the game again and again. He had to stop and then warm up again four different times. The Phillies finally lost 3–1 in a game that didn't end until 3:11 A.M.—7 hours and 36 minutes after it began.

With so many Astroturf fields, these endlessly delayed games were becoming commonplace. After this one, a suburban Philadelphia couple sued the Phillies, claiming it was cruel and unusual punishment to expect fans to sit through more than five hours of rain delays.

"There was nothing worse than those games," said Luzinski. "You'd sit and sit, get ready to play, and then sit some more," he said. "And it seemed like we had an awful lot of them in 1980."

Aside from the rain-delayed games, the Phillies played rapidly in 1980. Twelve games were finished in under two hours. More than half (83 games) took less than two hours and 30 minutes. Another 36 games took less than 2:40.

They were still three back on June 12 when Lerch lost to the Giants. It was the left-hander's eighth loss in ten decisions.

Meanwhile, before the games and in the clubhouse, they were reverting to some of their old habits. That had been the pattern in the Ozark years. They'd play cards instead of taking infield for a few days. Ozark would chastise them mildly. They'd reform for a few games only to quickly revert.

Green had a note installed on the wall where the lineup card was hung each day. It pointed out that anyone who cared to skip infield practice was welcome to—if they wrote a $100 check to the Child Guidance Clinic for each absence.

"Some of my guys are giving up on infield practice

already," complained Green. "I'm seeing some laziness from guys who need to work hard to be at their best. I've got guys who are throwing everything to Pete Rose on a bounce sitting out infield practice (Schmidt), guys who don't have great arms in the first place (Luzinski) missing the cutoff man. It's got me a little upset."

Schmidt responded by claiming that infield was one of baseball's many unnecessary anachronisms.

"Infield," explained "Professor" Schmidt, "consists of three soft groundballs, five-hoppers."

Say what you will about Green—and his players said plenty—but the guy usually sensed how and when to push buttons. The Phillies responded to this latest criticism by winning six straight. The problem was the manager never did locate a permanent "on" switch.

For the season's first five months, they required constant prodding. They needed a villain to get them going. When Green screamed or ripped them in the papers, it was him. If a pitcher fired at their heads, go get him. When writers criticized, it was them. When fans booed, they filled the role.

"We'd play good baseball for a week or so," said Green. "But it seems like every time we did, we'd fall right back again. If it wasn't for Carlton, we might have been out of it early that year."

The big left-hander looked nearly as spectacular as he had in 1972. He had 13 wins—and just two defeats—by June 22. On April 26, he threw an NL-record sixth one-hitter against St. Louis. In a June 27 loss to New York, Carlton passed Robin Roberts as the Phillies' strikeout king with 1,873 and moved ahead of Cy Young into ninth place all-time. On July 6, he passed Mickey Lolich's strikeout record for left-handers when he fanned number 2,833.

Carlton was in fantastic shape. His devotion to weights and rigid training schedules would help revolutionize baseball's fitness philosophy. If he had been a .500 pitcher, of course, everyone would have looked at him as a rice-pounding flake. But he was 35 and unhittable. That qualified him for role model status.

"The man just continues to amaze me every time he works out," said Hoefling. "He has recuperative powers beyond my comprehension."

The records were tumbling for Rose, too. On June 13 in San Diego, Rose had four hits to move past Honus Wagner into fifth place with 3,431.

But after taking the first three games of a West Coast trip, Philadelphia dropped eight of ten, including a June 28 twi-night doubleheader loss to the Mets. After that, they were right back where they were at the start of the month, three games out and three games over .500.

Green called a team meeting after the doubleheader, but remained relatively calm.

"It was not a stirring meeting," he said. "It was more like a stern reminder. In '76, '77, and '78, we blew guys out with raw talent. What's happening now is that the talent is equalized. Pittsburgh and Montreal have developed excellent ballclubs. St. Louis has a lot of offensive talent. Even the Mets are improving."

Some of the New York players found that "even the Mets" comment disparaging. They were further angered the next day when, after a 5–2 Philadelphia win, the Phils manager said, "We finally played like the Phillies, and they finally played like the Mets."

"Dallas has a tendency to let his ass overload his mouth," said Mets manager Joe Torre. "Maybe it's because every time he pitched, he got hit so hard."

"It's just like I always said," said Mets catcher John Stearns, "Dallas Green is a minor-league manager."

The pitching staff looked like it was going to get a big boost when Espinosa returned. In his first start, on July 4 in St. Louis, he allowed just two hits in eight shutout innings, though the Phils lost 1–0. But it was more illusion than portent. Espinosa's shoulder never fully healed. He would finish the year with a 3–5 mark, win just two games in 1981, vanish from baseball, and be dead from a heart attack in 1987.

Carlton won his 14th game on the final day of the first half. At the All-Star break, the inconsistent Phillies were 41–35, in second place. They trailed the first-place Expos by one game. They looked forward to rest and relaxation during the break.

They would be disappointed again.

◆ ◆ ◆

In baseball clubhouses in the 1970s and 1980s, amphetamines were as commonplace as coffee. Legal with a prescription, they were widely abused throughout America. Housewives took them to lose weight. College students used them to study all night. And athletes quickly discovered that a "greenie" before a game acted like artificial adrenaline.

Twenty years later Phillies players remain uncomfortable with the subject, but several will confirm that some of them used the pep pills.

"Nowadays people have a totally different view of (amphetamines)," said one member of the 1980 team. "You've got to remember back then they were all over the place. And they were perfectly legal if you had a prescription. You'd see all those skinny wives in the players' section, and you knew how they stayed that way. The fact that guys were taking them before games wasn't a shock. Nobody thought they were harmful or that they were going to get addicted. Hell, lots of people thought cocaine was OK then.

"It wasn't too much later, when you started to read about the (arrests) of all those guys on the Pirates and even some of the Kansas City guys we played against in the World Series, that baseball started to get the message that maybe this wasn't too smart. But guys kept taking them for years. Probably still do."

On July 8, during the All-Star break, the Phillies read it about themselves.

A story in the *Trenton* (New Jersey) *Times* reported that drug investigators suspected several Phillies of receiving amphetamines from a Reading, Pennsylvania, physician, later identified as Dr. Patrick Mazza.

It turned out that Mazza had written 23 prescriptions for the amphetamine Desoxyn between 1978 and 1980 in the names of several Phillies players and their wives. They eventually were identified as Carlton, Rose, Luzinski, Lerch, Christenson, McCarver, Jean Luzinski, and Sheena Bowa. Early stories erroneously implicated Bowa and Schmidt.

Mazza was a kind of unofficial physician for the Phillies Double A affiliate in Reading, an old textile-mill town about 55 miles northwest of Philadelphia. A third party had been getting the prescriptions filled at Reading pharmacies and passing them on to the ballplayers.

All those named denied having had any doctor-patient relationship with Mazza. None was ever charged. But at a 1981 hearing in which the case against Mazza was dropped, the doctor said he knew all the players named and cited specific reasons that each had wanted the pills—reasons ranging from loneliness to poor performance to weight control.

No one, it seemed, had much difficulty believing the Phillies used amphetamines. Fans pointed to Luzinski's sudden weight loss as an indication that he may have been on the diet pills. And a year earlier, in a *Playboy* interview, Rose had admitted that he occasionally used "greenies."

The news swirled with hurricane force for a few weeks, then dissipated as the pennant race intensified. Before the story played itself out, though, it helped to sour further the relationship between the Phillies and the local media.

"Yeah, there was a lot of turmoil that year," recalled Rose, who in addition to the drug trouble had gone through a divorce and a paternity suit early in his brief Phillies career. "But there's always some of that. Teams that win put it aside when they go between the lines. Look at Oakland. They won three straight World Series, and who had more turmoil than them?"

Chapter 6

An August Stumble, a Pittsburgh Rumble

You got to stop being so fucking cool. If you don't get that through your fucking minds, you're gonna be so fucking buried it ain't gonna be fucking funny.

DALLAS GREEN

Ten days into August they looked as dead as downtown Houston at dusk.

If sound tracks accompanied baseball seasons, then Verdi's "Requiem" would have been fitting for the Phillies' month that followed the All-Star break.

Bleak. Melancholic. Strangely compelling. You cried but couldn't turn away.

The 33 days between July 8, when the diet-pill dragnet was disclosed, and August 10, when they dropped a doubleheader in Pittsburgh, had left them severely wounded. The Phillies were in third place, six games behind the Pirates and Montreal. It remained only for their headstone to be carved. "Here lies the 1980 Phillies," it might have read. "Too good for their own good. Too angry. Too uncertain. Too late."

"After that Pittsburgh series, you couldn't find anyone who thought this team was going to win a world championship," said Stark, the *Inquirer*'s beat writer that year. "Everyone wrote them off."

All the unrest, all the unpleasant themes that had been simmering around them, burst into flame that month. One sportswriter noted that their clubhouse, a tense and sullen place even in the best of times, now seemed "filled with as much mirth as a cancer ward."

One hundred six games into the 1980 season and Phillies players had yet to buy into Green's "We Not I." For them, at that point, a more appropriate rallying cry would have been "Us Not Him."

Stung by the drug accusations, the Phillies retreated deeper into themselves. Even Green noticed. As the writers left his office following a home win against the Cubs, they hesitated for an instant. Not a single player was at his locker.

"I don't envy you guys your job," said Green to the writers. "That's a tough sell out there."

Fortunately for the Philadelphia media, the players' distaste for them soon was overwhelmed again by their dislike for the manager.

The odd collection of personalities on the Phillies—laid-back and loopy, erratic and eccentric, irritating and irascible, self-absorbed and snarling—made for a potentially volatile clubhouse.

"Every day when you walked through that door," said McGraw, "you wondered if this was going to be the day a riot broke out."

Mix in a scrutinizing press and vocal fans and it's a wonder United Nations peacekeepers weren't summoned to South Philadelphia that summer. When Green showed up, all the acrimony was pointed in his direction.

"I think Dallas eased some of that," said McGraw. "He

made some things so controversial, he had the guys so mad at him with some of the quotes that the dark cloud from over the clubhouse settled right over his door. It was probably one of the best things he did, although he might have lost a few friends on the team by doing so."

One of those he lost early was Luzinski. By late July, Luzinski was comparing Green to "the fucking Gestapo." Not long afterward Mount St. Green erupted with an ear-splitting roar in Pittsburgh. The pressure, so evident in their locker room, now seemed to have spilled onto the field. They followed the break by going 14–17 in their next 31 games.

On top of all this angst, as they entered the season's crucial stage, the Phillies were hurting. Schmidt, Bowa, Trillo, McGraw, McBride, Luzinski all missed time in July with injuries. Even that couldn't excuse their lackadaisical play during that stretch.

Batters missed pitches they normally crushed. Fielders made easy errors. They were coasting through losses. With 56 games remaining, their trademark, wrote the *Daily News*'s Ray Didinger, had become "slipping into defeat as if it were a lounge chair."

Bowa blamed it on the turmoil.

"Up until two or three weeks ago, I couldn't do anything," he said in mid-September when the Phillies had recovered. "I wasn't mentally in the game. Thoughts would go through my mind when the guy was in the windup. You can't play baseball like that."

After watching them lose a sixth straight game on July 23, 7–3 to the Reds at Cincinnati, former Phillies pitcher Jim Bunning, then a Kentucky state senator and a players agent, couldn't conceal his disgust. Bunning had thrown a perfect game for the team in 1964 and later managed in their farm system. But he couldn't bear to watch these pitiful performances.

"How can you stand to sit and watch these guys play every day?" he asked a Philadelphia writer in the Riverfront Stadium press box. "It's time to break this team up, start subtracting. You don't have to be a genius to figure out that if a team that has been together nine years hasn't done it by now, it's time to retool."

The trading deadline had come and gone. The Phillies still needed starting pitching. They needed power insurance in case Luzinski couldn't come back from the knee problems that had disabled him, in case Schmidt's groin pull lingered. Trillo, Smith, and McBride were hitting, but no one was driving them in.

The verbal warfare between Green and his players had flared up at times throughout the season as he continued to prod them with newsprint. They increasingly felt betrayed by the manager, as if some ancient bond had been snapped. He didn't care.

Green was different. Baseball's history was packed with unpopular managers, men whose hunger for victories turned them into little tyrants. John McGraw not only frequently challenged players to fight, but one day in Cincinnati the Giants manager challenged every fan in the ballpark. Leo Durocher didn't get the nickname "The Lip" because of collagen injections. His words stung, and many of his players disliked him intensely. Mauch screamed and yelled and had little patience with young players. On one messy occasion in Houston, he overturned the postgame buffet table, a display of temper that hit his hungry Phillies where it hurt.

But none of those managers used the newspapers nearly as often as Green to communicate their displeasure. In fact, most of his contemporaries had mastered the art of never saying anything critical in public. Even Billy Martin's worst blasts generally were reserved for his owner.

In baseball, this was the era of public relations not public floggings.

"There was a feeling among the players, I think, that this wasn't the way to do things," said Schmidt. "If you were going to preach togetherness, then you'd better practice it. If you had a problem with a player, call him in and behind closed doors read him the riot act. Don't take every dispute public"

What really bothered some players about Green's tactics was the fact that in his very first meeting with them that spring, he had told them, "We don't want to get into any shouting matches through the newspapers." It was as if the Three Stooges had vowed, "Look, whatever we do, we're not going to resort to slapstick."

In an ideal world, he might have meant it. But when the team labored through the first five months, he belabored them in print.

He and Owens had talked about that issue prior to the season. Like his manager, Owens felt the newspapers could help motivate a player or a team. This year, they had decided, there would be no whining to Carpenter or Owens as had happened under Ozark. Green had the authority to do what he pleased. If that meant bitching in the papers, fine.

"Hell, you can really get your message across that way," Owens said. "Now I'm not saying that you had to name names, but if you were unhappy, when the writers came in after the game, there was nothing wrong with telling them, 'Boy, I'm disappointed in our infield.'

"The player would know who you meant. The fans would know who you meant," he said.

Green, however, often had difficulty remaining vague. He named names.

The episode that eventually would ratchet up the feud several notches began after Lerch got shelled in a 13–11 loss to Pittsburgh on July 14.

"I'm about up to here with him," said Green. "I've tried everything to get him going. I need a more competitive pitcher out there."

Shy and surprisingly lacking in confidence for a major-leaguer, Lerch was popular among his teammates. Some of the Phillies veterans, particularly fellow pitchers like Reed and Lerrin LaGrow, didn't mind if Green attacked them in the press, but didn't think it right that the manager continually was on Lerch. The clubhouse buzz intensified.

LaGrow, a 32-year-old reliever who had been a free agent signee but fallen out of favor when he walked 17 in 39 innings, asked to speak to Green, pitching coach Starrette, and Owens.

"The pressure is getting to the guys," LaGrow told them, "the criticism, the singling guys out in the papers."

On July 17, when McGraw returned from the disabled list, LaGrow was released. He said he welcomed the move. Putting on the uniform in the Phillies clubhouse each day, he said, had become an unpleasant chore. He wasn't kidding. LaGrow never played again.

Then, several days later, during a loss in Atlanta, Lonnie Smith badly misplayed a ball. Backing him up, Maddox bobbled it and threw to the wrong base. Green went easy on Smith, who had accepted the blame, but had harsh words for Maddox.

Rehabilitating back in Philadelphia, Luzinski, a close friend of the outfielder's, fumed. On July 23, the same day Bunning suggested the Phillies be dismantled, Luzinski fired back at his manager. Green had been hypocritical in spring training, he told a newspaper columnist, when he suggested to his team that he wanted them to have fun.

"The minute the bell rang (at the start of the season) it changed a little. There are some sensitive guys who are getting hurt by all the screaming, getting singled out for one bad pitch or one bad play," Luzinski said, noting the comments about Lerch and Maddox. "He's got these signs all over the place that say 'We Not I,' and he wouldn't want the players yapping to the press about the mistakes he makes.

"I think he's hurting us. He's trying to be a fucking Gestapo. I stay at home and read his quotes and it really disappoints me. Dallas has said himself that he has some shortcomings, and one of them is his mouth."

Green responded by suggesting that Luzinski not read the newspapers. His real explosion was still a few weeks away.

"All I'm asking these guys to do is look in a mirror and see if they like what they see," Green said. "If they can handle our performance lately without doing some soul-searching then we're worse off than I think we are."

Asked how he thought the manager had reacted to the six-game losing streak, Schmidt's answer was dripping with not-so-subtle hints.

"Chuck Tanner has a different philosophy," said Schmidt of the Pirates' affable manager, "and maybe it's easy for him to have it. He's got the world champions. We don't know if their personality changes when they lose six in a row. Tanner probably tells them to turn up those tape players and says, 'Let's hear some noise! This ain't the end of the world.'"

Back home for a 12-game homestand, the Phillies split a doubleheader with the Braves. Atlanta manager Bobby Cox told Bowa that he had been reading the Philadelphia papers and it sounded like the Phillies were four games out with two to play. (Actually they were five out with 70 to play.)

In the Phillies' victory over Atlanta, Schmidt had hit his 260th homer, surpassing Del Ennis's club record. He used this occasion, too, to criticize the manager.

"The record doesn't mean a damn thing," said Schmidt.

"Dallas is trying to change this team's personality. He points out mistakes in the media instead of to us. But we're too big to let these things affect us."

The Phils would win six of their first eight at home, eight of 12 on the homestand, to climb back to within 3½ games of first place on August 7. Trillo was on fire, leading the league in hitting at .333 as late as July 20. McBride went 5-for-5 with three RBIs in a July 29 win over the Astros, raising his average to .312 and his RBI total to 61, second to Schmidt. Smith, his playing time increased by Luzinski's injury, had a batting average that was approaching .350.

After Carlton's 17th victory, a 3–2 win over the Cardinals in Philadelphia, the Phillies were off to Pittsburgh for a crucial four-game series. They had lost 11 of 15 there to the defending world champions.

But Three Rivers Stadium was about to get much more inhospitable.

◆ ◆ ◆

It was difficult to believe the clubhouse doors were made of steel, the walls of reinforced concrete. The reporters who stood in dark, tense silence outside the visiting clubhouse at Three Rivers Stadium on August 10 had all heard Green scream before. Hell, when the Phillies manager yelled, ships at sea picked him up. But this was something else.

The Phillies had just lost for a third straight game, 7–1 to Pittsburgh. It was an all-too-typical defeat for this struggling team. The freewheeling, physically imposing Pirates seemed to intimidate them. They were everything the Phillies were not— loose, relaxed, together.

Trillo had dropped a routine throw from Schmidt to kill a potential double play and instigate a Pirates rally. Bowa had thrown a ball away, even though bulky pitcher Don Robinson barely was moving toward first. Lerch had lost for a 13th time in 16 decisions. Phillies hitters were tentative. Green was not.

Triggered by the unusual volume, one of the writers clicked on his tape recorder. The device captured Green's profane verbal gusts so clearly, he might have been standing next to them. At that moment, they were glad he wasn't.

"This game isn't easy," Green screamed at his assembled club. "It's fucking tough, and we're fucking hurting with injuries. But you fucking guys got your fucking heads down. You got to stop being so fucking cool. If you don't get that through your fucking minds, you're gonna be so fucking buried it ain't gonna be fucking funny. Get the fuck up off your butts and go beat somebody! You're a fucking good baseball team. But you're not now. You can't look in the fucking mirror. You keep telling me you can do it, but you fucking give up. If you don't want to play, get the fuck in that office and tell me, 'I don't fucking want to play anymore!' Because if you feel that way, I don't want to play you. OK, let's go!"

The wall-rattling outburst was as much an outlet for Green's rising frustrations as it was an attempt at motivation.

"I used to like to give the manager a couple of minutes alone with the team after games," said Owens, who was one of the first GMs to travel full-time with his club. "So I sat upstairs in the press box awhile. When I got down there, the writers were waiting outside, and they looked like they had just seen a ghost. I asked them what had happened, and they said, 'You won't believe it. It was unbelievable.' So, I'm thinking, 'Wow! What the hell did he say?'"

The players had sensed it coming since the first day of spring training. When Green had finished, some sat quietly by their lockers. A few whispered their reactions to a teammate.

Some changed their jerseys and went out for the next game as if nothing had happened.

Emotions were still raw. During the Phillies' second-game loss to the Pirates, 4–1, which dropped them six games back of both Pittsburgh and Montreal, Green and Reed squared off in the dugout. The two large men were face-to-face after the reliever had given up a pair of runs and been yanked.

"A lot of managers have yelled and shouted between games of a doubleheader," said Green. "But when I went jaw-to-jaw with Ronnie, I was kind of anxious to see how the guys would handle it. There was a chance it could really hurt the ballclub. But we came out of it, and I gave the guys credit. They put the thing behind and went after the season."

Looking back on a championship season, the tendency is to search for turning points. A stunning late-inning rally. A walk-off home run against an ace closer. A team meeting. For the Phillies, Green's outburst and Owens's subsequent soliloquy usually get the credit. And, after the Game 2 loss, there was an initial burst. The Phillies won nine of their next 11 games to close within 1½ games of the fading Pirates on August 21.

A day later, in Chicago, the players called a team meeting. That, insisted some, had more of an impact than Green's harsh words.

"We lost those four straight to the Pirates, and we left there, and everybody wrote us off," said Reed. "Then we got together in Chicago—just the players—and we said, 'Hey, let's don't go (back) to fourth place. We're better than a fourth-place club. Forget all the other stuff and play for ourselves. Get together as a team, but play for us.'

"We had a meeting, 'The hell with Dallas. The hell with the coaching staff. Let's win it for us.' And it seemed like we came together after that. It was a very brief sort of thing, but we turned it around. That was the closest I've ever seen guys come together as a team."

Certainly these Phillies did seem to need an ax to grind. Green's tirade gave them one. The players' meeting probably narrowed their focus into the kind of "Us vs. Them" outlook that sometimes works in sports. And Owens's words probably stung them since the GM obviously cared so much.

"You know, probably each one pushed them in their own way," said Owens. "Whatever the cause was, the bottom line is they got their act together and played tremendous ball down the stretch of that season, and it carried right over in the post-season."

The truth about that Phillies turnaround no doubt was more prosaic.

Wrigley Field, often an elixir for him, brought Schmidt's bat to life and he wouldn't cool off again. Schmidt homered nine times in September, and clubbed four more in October. Ruthven regained his consistency to give them a solid No. 2 starter. At last McGraw came off the DL and was practically unhittable into the play-offs. And both Pittsburgh and Montreal cooled off.

Remember, while they did win nine of 11 after leaving Pittsburgh, the Phillies followed that streak with six losses in ten games, including the two sloppy defeats in San Diego that set Owens off. As September began, Philadelphia was just a half-game behind at 68–60.

"The Pope's meeting backed up what I had told them," said Green. "Everyone there knew I had the hammer."

◆ ◆ ◆

A silent tension hung in the air like smoke as the Phillies made the short flight from Pittsburgh to Chicago that August

10. Something, they sensed, needed to happen, and soon. Wrigley Field, with its pitching-poor inhabitants, its often friendly breezes and inviting distances, was as good a place as any.

The Phillies blew a big lead in the rain-delayed opener, and the game was tied at 5–5 when darkness forced its suspension. When the game resumed the following day, Schmidt, who had homered earlier, slammed a two-run triple in the 15th inning as the Phils won 8–5.

"If we had blown that . . . game," Green said at season's end, "it could have been downhill for us."

Then Schmidt homered and singled in the regularly scheduled game, a 5–2 victory.

"It's time for him to hit," said Green. "He's been shut down pretty good for a real long time. He's worked real hard at correcting some technical things, and now it looks like it's time to let his talent take over."

Dick Tidrow beat Ruthven 2–1 the following day, but the Phillies went into New York and swept a five-game series. Carlton's 20th victory, 4–3 over L.A. on August 27, gave them a disappointing 4–5 homestand against the West Coast clubs. And on August 28, they flew to the West Coast in third place, 2½ games behind Montreal, 2 back of Pittsburgh.

Chapter 7

A Divided Team Wins a Division

I have noticed that when chickens quit quarreling over their food they often find that there is enough for all of them.

DON MARQUIS

Suppose quantum physics one day unlocks the door to time travel. You are a Phillies fan lusting to return to 1980's regular season. But you can afford only a one-day ticket. Don't bother checking with a travel agent. Pick September 29.

On that long-ago Monday night in South Philadelphia, you will witness perfect examples of that team's two most compelling traits—the grit of a champion, and the sort of pettiness and animosity normally associated with soccer parents and presidential debates.

During the hours between 3 P.M. and midnight, you will:

- Read a starting lineup that leaves three key veterans stewing on the bench.
- See the centerfielder who dropped a fly ball in the sun a day earlier collar a writer and angrily blame him for his benching because he wrote that the centerfielder dropped a fly ball in the sun a day earlier.

- Hear the Phillies shortstop blast the manager on his radio show an hour before a crucial game.
- Listen as Philadelphia fans boo the home team viciously, even though they are a half-game out of first with a week left in the season.
- Watch as, later, the same shortstop shoots a middle finger at those fans, then obscenely maligns them.
- Listen as their manager, after a stirring victory, accuses some of his own players of "rooting against us" and vows to break up his team.
- And, until they win with a stunning 15th-inning rally, you'll be trying to figure out how the hell this psychotic Phillies team ever won a World Series three weeks later.

The events that led to Moody Monday can be traced back to Green's benching, at various times throughout September, of Boone, Luzinski, and Maddox. That afternoon, when Bowa saw all three of his pals missing from that night's lineup—replaced by Lonnie Smith, Keith Moreland, and Del Unser—he seethed.

Maddox had seen the lineup card, too. He thought he knew why his name wasn't there and went looking for the *Inquirer*'s Stark. Maddox told the writer he wanted to talk and escorted him to a small room off the clubhouse.

"He was very angry," said Stark, "and accusing me of a lot of things that amazed me."

Maddox contended that by mentioning his misplay so prominently, Stark had prompted Green to bench him.

"He manages for the press," explained the centerfielder.

Meanwhile, Bowa didn't have to wait long to vent his unhappiness. The ten-year veteran hosted an evening sports segment on radio station WWDB-FM. Guess what that night's topic was? (Hint: It wasn't Flyers' training camp.)

"Dallas has said he is going to let the veterans go to the hilt," Bowa began. "To me, this is not letting the veterans go to the hilt. If he's going to let Lonnie and Keith play (that night against the Cubs), then I'm sure he's going to let them play against the Expos in Montreal (the final weekend of the season).

"He can't sit down Boonie and Luzinski for four days and then when we go against Montreal say, 'OK, go get 'em again.' In order for them to find their batting stroke or find their batting eye, they have to play every day. If they're not going to play every day, don't just throw them in against the Montreal Expos. Dallas is trying to shake things up, which is very understandable, but on the other hand he's talking out of both sides of his mouth by saying he wants to stay with the veterans."

And by the way, fans, he might have added, you might want to hold off on those World Series ticket applications.

That night's crowd was relatively small (21,127) but hostile. Some had heard Bowa's commentary on their way to the stadium. Others didn't appreciate how the Phillies had dropped two of three at home to Montreal over the weekend or how they kept squandering opportunities to put away the Cubs. And when, in the 15th, an error helped Chicago take a 5–3 lead, they howled like welfare activists at a Ronald Reagan rally.

"They gave up on us tonight," Green said of the fans.

Christenson was superb until Chicago touched him for a pair of runs in the seventh to go ahead 3–2. The Phillies tied it in the bottom of the inning, the last runs scored until the 15th.

With a runner at first and one out in that inning, Mick Kelleher slapped what looked like a double play ground ball back at Noles. The reliever turned and fired, but his throw sailed past Bowa. The runners ended up at first and third, and Green called for Warren Brusstar.

Scott Thompson's sacrifice fly made it 4–3, and Carlos Lez-cano's double over Maddox's head in center increased Chicago's lead to 5–3. As the Phillies ran toward their dugout at inning's end, the angry fans let them have it.

Thank God for Doug Capilla.

The 28-year-old Hawaiian-born reliever may have saved the Phillies season. He walked Smith and Rose, who had three RBIs to end a 4-for-36 slump, to start the bottom of the 15th. Then he wild-pitched them up a base, which proved to be a crucial miscue when McBride's subsequent grounder produced not a double play but only one out and a fourth Philadelphia run.

Dennis Lamp, scheduled to start the following night, came in from the bullpen to face Schmidt. The Phillies slugger popped up for the second out, and the boos began anew.

"Christ," thought Bowa at short, his tiny fuse growing even shorter. "The guy has 44 homers and he's been hot as hell and they boo him! That ain't right."

Up came Maddox. Green had inserted him earlier, and this was his second at bat. He singled to tie the score. Bowa walked before Trillo, on a 1–1 pitch, lined the game-winning single to center.

Phillies players surrounded Maddox as he crossed the plate. The vocal remnants of the crowd screamed in delight. Running to the dugout, Bowa answered their cheers with the middle finger on his right hand. He hadn't cooled off any ten minutes later when the writers entered the clubhouse. Bowa hadn't been talking to the media since the diet-pill headlines, but he wanted them to hear this.

"Worst fucking fans in the world!" he screamed. "Front-running motherfuckers!"

Three weeks later, the night before he would call those same fans the "greatest in the world," Bowa insisted he was merely serving as a spokesman for his less vocal teammates.

"We walked in here, and 25 guys wanted to say the fans were brutal," he said. "None of them wanted to say it (out loud). So I said it."

Curiously, McGraw had foreseen this kind of trouble. In a breakfast interview with Stan Hochman, a *Daily News* columnist, early in September, the reliever lamented the deteriorating connection between Philadelphia's fans and players.

"Here in Philly, for whatever reason, there's a terrible relationship between the fans and the players," he said. "The fans make it very difficult for the players to enjoy their presence. And the players make it difficult, through their indifference, for the fans to enjoy them."

Bowa's postgame diatribe was just the beginning of the fun that night in Club Chaos's Crazed Clubhouse.

Green, who might have been expected to revel in the dramatic victory, instead sounded like a man who had been listening to the radio.

"I got a feeling we're not all together in this thing," he began cryptically. "I would be surprised if there aren't a few guys out there who are rooting against us. For the last two weeks, I've watched these guys very closely, and it's almost back to the same old thing, the 'We're-gonna-do-it-our-way' type of thing."

Asked to elaborate on these allegations of sabotage, Green went on:

"It's the little things they continue to do, things they know piss me off. I'd say 90 percent of the guys care, they want to win. The rest, well, they can look in the mirror."

He continued, promising he would do everything in his power to make sure that the other 10 percent was somewhere else next season.

Somehow Schmidt, never quick to notice wind shifts in the clubhouse, was able to overlook the night's off-the-field events. He later pointed instead—perhaps naively, perhaps correctly—to the significance of the comeback.

"That was the first time we felt like things really came together for us as a team," said Schmidt. "In the past, it seemed that my teammates couldn't pick me up, and the burden of failure would be even greater on me. But this time Garry Maddox came off the bench to tie the game and later Manny Trillo won it."

Still, the team's best player might have been expected to question the wisdom of starting the season's final week with internecine potshots and fan-directed profanities.

More than a year into Green's tumultuous tenure, not much had changed. Guys whined and complained. Green ripped them in the press. Fans booed.

Something had to give.

◆ ◆ ◆

The following morning Green got an invitation to Carpenter's office on the Vet's fourth level. The owner nearly had choked on his yogurt when he read about the nasty night's events. Mouth-to-mouth combat wasn't the *Spalding Guide* formula for a contender at the end of September.

"Ruly asked me 77 questions, and I answered 76 of them satisfactorily," Green explained later. "I told him I don't think he understands totally what's going on down here."

The Harvard philosophy department would have difficulty decoding the psychological muddle bubbling in the basement of Veterans Stadium.

"God dammit, I'm not going to get into a pissing contest with Larry Bowa," said Green. "If I was ever going to open up on Larry Bowa, he'd never play another inning in Philadelphia—and that's official. I'm in this for one fucking thing, and that's to win. I'm beyond the point of caring about people's feelings.

"I could quit. That's what Danny Ozark did after seven years. He just quit. He threw it over to them. He said, 'Here, do it your way.' Now I can see why. . . ."

Boone, Luzinski, and Maddox were back in Green's lineup that night. But Maddox still fumed. During batting practice, he asked Bobby Wine to tell Green that the hand he had jammed in Pittsburgh two weeks earlier hurt him and he couldn't swing the bat. This came as a surprise to Wine, who had watched Maddox deliver the game-tying hit the night before.

Soon Unser's name was back in the lineup. Maddox later claimed he hadn't pulled himself out, but only informed Wine so that Green could make the ultimate decision. Green disagreed, saying the outfielder told Wine he couldn't play.

Two decades later Maddox conceded that he had been wrong.

"I let our feud get to me more than it should have," he said. And that wasn't even the night's most interesting sidelight. Bowa ought to have made the zero in his No. 10 a bull's-eye. Fans responded to his criticism with increased outrage of their own. He couldn't take a step without hearing them.

"You can punch a writer here and rate a standing ovation and second-guess a manager with impunity," wrote Conlin in the next day's *Daily News*. "But tell a Philadelphia fan he's a front-runner and you'd have less chance of getting clawed milking a panther. I mean how can you front-run in a town which claims two National League pennants in a century which is four-fifths shot?"

Somehow Bowa managed two hits, an RBI, a run scored,

and a great defensive play in a 14–2 Phillies victory. Schmidt homered. Luzinski homered. Boone, who had been 0-for-22, had a pair of hits. And Bystrom won his fifth game without a loss.

On October 1, Carlton two-hit the Cubs in the third of the four-game series. Schmidt, on fire now, belted his 45th homer. Walk completed the sweep the next night, 4–2, as Schmidt homered again.

With three games remaining, they were dead even with Montreal, which is exactly where they were headed that weekend.

◆ ◆ ◆

September had begun in a haze for them.

Early on September 1, Maddox informed Green that he wanted to address the club and apologize for missing those two fly balls in San Diego. The manager told him that wouldn't be necessary. He could have added, "Because Pope is about to ream you and Bowa out in front of the whole club."

Minutes before the month's first game, the Phillies sat in Candlestick Park's visitors' clubhouse and listened to their general manager's angry words. Then they went out to face the Giants. San Francisco had beaten them in six of their first nine meetings. They couldn't afford to lose another series, but they were still stinging from Owens's lecture.

Somehow, when they walked off the field less than three hours later, they were a first-place team. They had managed a 6–4 victory that left them with the thinnest of division leads, .001 percentage points. Carlton, though again not at his best, won his 21st game. You could hear the sigh of relief all the way to Marin County.

"I was proud of them that day," said Owens. "They could

have had their tails between their legs after some of the things I said, but they responded. And it didn't hurt any that we had Carlton pitching."

The Phillies swept the Giants but lost two of three games in Los Angeles to drop back into second place. They stayed there for most of the month. And anyone who thought the bickering and controversy would end after Green's and Owens's outbursts didn't know very much about the 1980 Phillies.

The newest round of squabbling began in San Francisco. Maddox figured he was being punished by Green when he was benched for the entire series against the Giants and two of the four games in Los Angeles.

"I had been used to coming to the ballpark prepared to play," Maddox said. "That year, I never knew from one game to the next, especially in September. I'd read about my status in the newspapers."

September 3 was a typically frosty night at Candlestick Park. Freezing on the bench in the middle innings, Maddox told third-base coach Lee Elia he was going to the clubhouse, which was in rightfield and not connected to the dugout as in most stadiums.

He used the rest room and got a cup of coffee. Meanwhile, Green had wanted to insert him for defense in the close game. The manager's blood pressure approached Rose's lifetime batting average when he couldn't locate the centerfielder. The outburst was over by the time Maddox, carrying the coffee, returned to the dugout.

The next day in Los Angeles, teammates told Maddox how angry Green had been. The outfielder confronted the manager and informed him he had gotten permission from Elia.

"It got smoothed over," said Maddox.

◆ ◆ ◆

The 1980 Phillies roster was crowded with future Hall of Famers and players just a notch or two below that level.

Carlton and Schmidt were at their peaks. Rose was knocking over records like carnival Kewpie dolls. Bowa, Boone, and Maddox kept setting defensive marks and winning Gold Gloves. McBride, Trillo, and Luzinski were hardly average players.

So it sounds almost preposterous to suggest that the one player who was most responsible for the Phillies winning their first World Series was Marty Bystrom.

If the rookie right-hander with the fright-wig hair had not gone 5–0 following his September call-up, it's nearly impossible to envision a scenario in which the Phillies would have won the NL East.

Bystrom had graduated from high school in southern Florida without attracting any big-league attention. He was a free agent when the Phillies signed him off the Miami Dade Junior College team in 1977.

Maturing physically and as a pitcher, Bystrom won 13 games at Spartanburg, and Green and Owens watched him closely in the Florida Instructional League that fall.

"That was in '78 and we figured he'd be in the big leagues real soon," said Owens. "He threw four pitches for strikes. When we were down in Florida, he threw a shutout that had our heads spinning."

Bystrom likely would have made the club in 1980, but he had injured a leg that spring. On September 1, he was called up as bullpen insurance or, at best, a spot starter. But when Christenson's balky groin acted up, the rookie moved into the rotation.

"I was just a rookie trying to do whatever I could to help

the Phillies win," he said. "I kind of tried to stay in the background because Ron Reed had told us rookies were meant to be seen and not heard."

In retrospect, especially given how disappointing his career turned out, it's easy to point out that Bystrom's five victories came against the Cardinals, Mets, and Cubs, the fourth-, fifth-, and sixth-place teams in the NL East.

But they came in September. The Phillies were either in first or second place, never up or down by more than 1½ games, in each of his five starts. Plus, this was Philadelphia, home to more ghosts than Amityville. The George Washington Elementary School nine would have been a challenge for them.

"There have been lots of other guys who come up in September and win four or five games for a team going nowhere," said Schmidt. "The thing that makes what Marty did so incredible is that we were in a real dogfight (for first place in the division). Every time he went out there, it was a huge game.

"I know he was only with us in September, but you could have made a real strong case that he deserved Rookie of the Year."

The Phils trailed the Expos by a half-game when Bystrom shut out the Mets 5–0 in his debut. They were a game back when he beat St. Louis 8–4 on September 14. The Cardinals runs came off the bullpen and until Bystrom allowed a two-run homer to Dave Kingman in Chicago on September 20, he had a string of 20 consecutive scoreless innings. Philadelphia, behind the Expos by 1½ games, won that game, too, 7–3.

Philadelphia led Montreal by a half-game on September 25 when Bystrom stymied the Mets again, 2–1, for his fourth victory. Finally, on September 30, the day after Moody Monday, a composed Bystrom coasted to a 14–2 triumph over the Cubs that left the Phillies a half-game out.

By then, with Smith and Moreland playing as much as some of the veterans and with Walk and Bystrom in the rotation, Green didn't need further vindication of his master plan to stir the pot on this veteran-laden team by liberally mixing in rookies. But Bystrom offered some anyway.

"Dallas," said Bystrom, "gave the young guys a chance. A lot of the guys would never have gotten the same shot had Danny Ozark been the manager. With Dallas they got the shot, and they did the job."

Two days after Bystrom's fifth victory, Walk's 11th win gave the Phillies a sweep of the Cubs in their final regular-season home game. Schmidt hit his 46th homer as they won for the 49th time in 81 games at the Vet that summer.

If, as Bowa said, Phillies fans were the worst in the world, there were at least an awful lot of them. The team's attendance wound up at 2,651,650, despite several months of lackluster baseball.

Now, with the Phillies and Expos both at 89–70, the Phils prepared to leave for Montreal and a three-game season-ending series.

The 23,806 fans at that Thursday night win over the Cubs were, despite another long rain delay, perhaps the most upbeat of any that season. They prayed they would see the Phillies again.

◆   ◆   ◆

It was after midnight when the team's charter to Montreal took off. As players and coaches settled into their seats, they appeared as relaxed as they had been in a long time.

"It was just a personal thing," said Gross, "but we had the feeling that they had no chance."

A light rain was falling less than an hour and a half later as the charter touched down at Mirabelle Airport in Montreal. Traveling secretary Eddie Ferenz, himself a native Canadian, had arranged for the weary team to skip customs by promising airport workers tickets to the series.

For one of the few times in the Expos' history, hockey-mad Montreal quivered with baseball excitement that weekend. Young and talented, with stars like Andre Dawson, Warren Cromartie, Steve Rogers, Larry Parrish, Ron LeFleur, and Gary Carter, Montreal teetered joyfully on the edge of its first postseason.

A week earlier in Philadelphia, the Expos had won two of three and laid the groundwork for the ugly events that Monday night at Veterans Stadium.

McBride's ninth-inning home run had given the Phillies a 2–1 win in the opener of that earlier series, earning the right-fielder a thunderous curtain call from the Veterans Stadium crowd and pushing the Phillies 1½ games ahead of the Expos. Then they missed a huge opportunity to put Montreal away when Scott Sanderson beat Carlton 4–3 the following night.

The rubber game was Sunday, its starting time delayed to 3:05 for national TV. Rogers and the Expos led it 2–1 in the sixth when Maddox and the sun had another interesting encounter.

Montreal had runners at first and third when Chris Speier smoked a Dickie Noles pitch to left-center. The late-afternoon glare and shadows made picking up a line drive difficult. Maddox chased after it and caught up. Unlike at San Diego, he had his sunglasses on. But they were on the bottom of his cap's visor, and the centerfielder never flipped them down.

He lost the ball. Both runners scored on the resulting triple. Montreal's 5–1 victory put them back in first place by a half-game.

"I don't think having the sunglasses down would have made any difference," said Maddox.

"All I know is when I'm out in the sun, I can see better with sunglasses," said Green.

Now, in Montreal, sun wouldn't be a problem. The forecast called for a gloomy weekend —unless you were a baseball fan.

When Schmidt awoke in his Hyatt Regency room on October 3, he felt as if a Zamboni had run over his head. His throat stung. Congestion made breathing tough. He was afraid to take his temperature.

Schmidt didn't say anything, not that anyone would have expected him to at this stage of the season. He decided against asking for antibiotics. It had been his experience that feeling lousy sometimes helped you focus. Since all you could think about was how bad you felt, the distractions often vanished.

His sacrifice fly off Sanderson in the first inning quickly stilled the frenzied, singing crowd of 57,121 at Olympic Stadium. Then he homered off the Montreal right-hander in the sixth to give Ruthven a 2–0 lead. The home run was Schmidt's 47th, tying Eddie Mathews's record for NL third basemen. It was his third in three days, his eighth in two weeks.

But when Dawson's RBI in the bottom of the inning halved the Phillies advantage, Green brought in Sparky Lyle. After trying to land the ex-Yankee left-hander for the past few seasons, Owens finally got him on September 13. He wouldn't be eligible for postseason, but in big games like this, he gave Green some experienced bullpen insurance.

Lyle held the fort down until the eighth when McGraw entered. The wisecracking reliever was not just in a zone, he was in another world. After coming off the disabled list July 17, McGraw would permit just three earned runs in his next 52 innings.

This time he struck out five of the six batters he faced to preserve Ruthven's 17th victory and give the Phillies a one-game lead with just two to play.

"I peaked in Montreal," McGraw said. "There's no way I can pitch any better. I flash back on that all the time. I see hitters looking at pitches and swinging and missing at pitches that were as perfect as I could throw them—locationwise, rotationwise, deliverywise."

Now the Expos had to win the final two games. Manager Dick Williams liked their chances on Saturday, when their ace, Rogers, would oppose Christenson.

◆　◆　◆

Montreal's 1976 Olympic experience had been in many ways a disaster. Tourists stayed away. The city lost millions. And though Olympic Stadium was built to have a dome, local officials never seemed to have sufficient money or will to put it in place.

So when Saturday dawned with heavy rainfall, the Phillies, hoping to clinch and rest their regulars Sunday, were downcast. The last thing they wanted was a rainout.

"No way we're going to be able to play today," said Bowa, "and I don't like the idea of a doubleheader tomorrow either."

Players and club officials roamed the clubhouse nervously that morning and afternoon. After a delay of three hours and ten minutes, the game finally began at 5:25 P.M. It would be worth the wait.

The Phillies would commit five errors in the game. They collected 17 hits, but squandered nearly every scoring opportunity. They ran the bases like a T-ball team. A two-run single by Luzinski turned into an inning-ending double play when both he and Schmidt were caught.

Going into the ninth, they trailed Montreal by a run, 4–3. Woodie Fryman, a left-hander who had pitched in Philadelphia a decade earlier, walked Rose to start the inning. He got McBride and Schmidt on ground balls. Boone was next.

The veteran catcher, two for his last 25, had been benched in favor of Moreland when the game began. That had happened often in September. This time, he lined a high fastball into centerfield, and the game was tied. With extra catchers available— September call-ups Don McCormack and Tim McCarver, activated from the announcer's booth so he could become one of the rare players to have performed in four different decades— Green pinch-ran for Boone.

McGraw, practically automatic at this stage, struck out two Expos in the ninth and retired the third batter on a foul pop-up. He and Stan Bahnsen, another veteran reliever Owens had coveted, kept it scoreless through ten.

Rose's single started the 11th. With one out, Schmidt, maybe the hottest hitter in baseball, strutted to the plate. McCormack, whose major-league career would consist of five at bats and no base hits, was on deck. Though an intentional walk would have pushed Rose into scoring position, it still seemed like a no-brainer for Williams.

The Expos manager elected to pitch to the Phillies third baseman. Bahnsen fell behind 2–0 and grooved a fastball. Schmidt's 48th homer sailed deep into the leftfield grandstands.

His teammates tumbled toward home plate to greet him. Schmidt even smiled briefly as he slapped hands with Rose at home plate, before returning to his typical passionless demeanor.

McGraw retired Carter, Cromartie, and Parrish in order, and remarkably, the Phillies had won their fourth division title in five years.

"Mike Schmidt wins the game with McCormack coming up," said Bowa later. "We're out of players. I'll be damned if I'm going to let Mike Schmidt beat me when there's a kid coming up next. But not one thing was written in the papers up there. I guarantee you, if that happened in Philadelphia, we would have been picked apart."

Somehow, this season of headaches and headlines had led again to the play-offs. Now they would come under national scrutiny. There would be questions about their battles with Green, the fans, each other. As the Phillies doused themselves with beer and champagne that rainy night, no one expected the turmoil to stop.

"The only way to put a damper on this stuff," said Schmidt, "is to scrape out a division title and a play-off title and a World Series title."

Chapter 8

The Greatest Series Ever

What I remember about Houston was that the din was like a smoke-filled room. It was like the noise laid around your eyes.

PAUL OWENS

There may never have been a more typical Phillies fan than Harvey Moody.

A resident of suburban Warminster, Moody watched the Astros defeat the Dodgers in Monday's one-game play-off for the National League West title. Knowing then that Houston would be the Phillies opponent when the 1980 NL Championship Series opened Tuesday night, October 7, at Veterans Stadium, he journeyed to South Philadelphia. Ticket lines were two blocks long. He waited and waited, reading the papers, munching on a hoagie. When he finally reached the window, one ticket remained. The fact that it was an obstructed-view seat hadn't lessened its $15 price. Still, Moody gladly bought it.

A *Philadelphia Daily News* reporter, gathering facts for a story on postseason enthusiasm in the city, approached and asked the lucky purchaser if he thought the Phillies were going to beat the Astros. If this had been anyplace else and Moody a partisan of any other team, he might have been giddy at his own good fortune, blindly optimistic about the Phillies' chances. This, however, was Philadelphia.

"Nah," he said, "they're lousy under pressure."

That's how it was. Deep inside, these fans longed to give their hearts fully. But because they had been hurt so often, they held back. Real Phillies fans would never predict anything positive. That way, when the team disappointed them again, they could act tough and say they knew it all along.

While Moody was apprehensive, the Phillies were not. Publicly, they claimed it didn't matter if they met Houston or L.A. Privately, they prayed for the Astros. Green offered silent testimony to those feelings when, watching the one-game playoff for the NL West title in the Phils' clubhouse, he pumped his fist enthusiastically when Houston took a 2–0 lead.

Green had been around the Phillies for more than 30 years, and he just had a hunch things would be different this year. There was something like destiny at work. He had felt that way during those last terrible days of the 1964 season, too, only in reverse.

This team finally had exhibited some of the character Green was always harping about, scrapping for a division title after coasting to three others. And this time they wouldn't have to face the Dodgers and all the psychological baggage that matchup would have implied.

L.A. had beaten them in the 1977 and 1978 play-offs, and those defeats were recalled painfully in the clubhouse and in the city. No Dodgers meant one less historical hurdle to leap.

"We're better than those Phillies teams were," said Rose, always the one to disconnect this team from its terrible tradition. "The pitching is better, and I think the bench is better."

There was a statistical basis for optimism, too. Philadelphia had won 9 of 12 against Houston in 1980. The Astros weren't a team that was going to pummel you offensively very often. They hit just 75 home runs that year, 11th in the league.

They tended to manufacture runs. Their best hitters were left-handed, and that wouldn't help them if they had to face Carlton twice. Most importantly, they had to fly in from the West Coast late Monday night and open the series Tuesday.

"You got a team coming from a four-game trip (at the end of the regular season) to what they're going through in L.A.," said Rose, "and they don't even get to go home. That's not how you like to approach a play-off, going from the West Coast to the East Coast."

Playing in the Astrodome, Houston was built around its pitching. In midseason, the Astros had lost one of baseball's most dominant pitchers, J. R. Richard, who had suffered a career-ending stroke. But they did have Nolan Ryan and knuckleballer Joe Niekro, a 20-game winner. Their 3.10 staff ERA was the best in baseball.

The Phillies knew Ryan would be a factor in this series. Actually, he had a somewhat disappointing first season back in his home state. His record was only 11–10 with a 3.35 ERA, and he had just 200 strikeouts. While the Phils had beaten him twice, they all recalled his 10-strikeout shutout on May 16 as an example of how overpowering he could be.

Since Houston's rotation and bullpen were much deeper than Philadelphia's, Owens badly wanted Bystrom on his post-season roster.

The rookie seemed oblivious to pressure. But he was a September call-up and, as such, ineligible. Owens and Green both preferred the rookie to Nino Espinosa or Randy Lerch. Espinosa had been hurt much of the year and, while he was eligible at season's end, had lost considerable velocity.

That Sunday in Montreal, Green and Owens hinted to reporters that they planned to seek a roster exemption for Bystrom by convincing league officials Espinosa was hurt. Espinosa read about it back in Philadelphia the next day, reacted angrily, and was summoned for a meeting. Eventually, the club convinced Espinosa and NL president Chub Feeney that he couldn't pitch. Bystrom took his spot.

They would have liked to use Lyle, too, but that was impossible. So, needing another left-handed reliever, they preferred Saucier to the erratic Lerch and made that switch.

"Randy took it hard," said Green. "He'll probably rip me in a few days."

The manager was used to it. He had been shuffling his lineup for much of the season, even in the final week, and many of the veterans— Boone, Maddox, Luzinski—resented it. Green enjoyed keeping that trio on edge. He hated their normally placid demeanors. Benching them occasionally changed that. Now, asked about them the day before Game 1, the manager replied, "Boonie will catch."

What about Luzinski?

"Boonie will catch."

What about Maddox?

"Boonie will catch."

◆ ◆ ◆

Anyone who thought the division title healed all the Phillies' wounds wasn't watching closely during the introductions before Game 1 of the National League Championship Series.

Carlton, warming up in the bullpen, had been the last of the Phillies lineup introduced to the Veterans Stadium crowd that night of October 7. The three players closest to home plate were the eighth-, seventh-, and sixth-place hitters—Boone, Bowa, and Maddox.

Then announcer Dan Baker read, "Phillies manager . . . Dallas Green." Green clapped his hands while running from the dugout to the first-base line. As he neared them, Bowa and Maddox turned their heads to the left, gazing up the line toward first base. Snubbed, the manager veered toward Boone. The catcher was stuck. He extended an obviously reluctant hand, and they shook.

"Meant nothing," said Green of the incident.

Actually, it meant that, even in the postseason, "We Not I" was just a sign on a clubhouse wall.

The Phillies hadn't won an NLCS game at home in six tries, but a record crowd of 65,233 showed up anyway on a cold and damp Tuesday night. Hoping for the best, the spectators were ready for the worst.

The Phillies' riveting September, capped by the memorable Saturday game in Montreal, hadn't entirely altered Philadelphians' attitudes. During pregame introductions, four of the home team's nine starters—Boone, Luzinski, Maddox, and especially Bowa—were booed.

"It was good natured," said Bowa. "There were a lot of cheers mixed in."

Getting in on the hands of Philadelphia hitters on that chilly night, Ken Forsch was outpitching Carlton, who seemed uncomfortable after six days' rest.

Houston led 1–0 when Rose began the home sixth inning by beating out a high chopper to short. McBride struck out and Forsch got Schmidt on a fly ball to center—prompting more boos. Luzinski then walked to the plate.

He had looked pathetic in his first two at bats, striking out on checked swings in the first and popping up feebly to short in the fourth. This time the big leftfielder worked the count full and looked for a fastball. Forsch provided one, down and in. Luzinski's short stroke connected. The ball soared into the 300 level in leftfield, just below the "Bull Ring," a section of seats Luzinski had purchased for needy kids.

"It was incredible because that was kind of the way the season began for me," said Luzinski. "I had started it with a big home run at home, then I got hurt and there was all that other stuff that went on. Now, in the NLCS, it was like starting over again."

The Phillies led 2–1 and, buoyed by the prospect of seeing the team's first home play-off win in over six decades, the huge crowd exploded.

Knowing he'd probably need him again in this series, Green yanked Carlton for a pinch hitter with two outs and Maddox on third in the seventh. Gross's flared single to left, the first of many big hits the bench would collect in the next two weeks, made it 3–1. McGraw threw two more scoreless innings, and the Phillies, with unusual ease, led the NLCS.

◆ ◆ ◆

Carlton had become the first Phils pitcher since Grover Cleveland Alexander to win a postseason game at home. But the euphoria didn't last long. The Astros rallied to win Game 2 7–4 in ten innings, and Conlin's story in the next day's *Daily News* started this way: "The Phillies' latest descent into postseason hell began. . . ."

When it came to the Phillies, hell, apparently, was never more than a day away.

The locals found someone to blame for their unexpected dismay. Lee Elia, the native Philadelphian who was the team's third-base coach, had held the potential winning run at third in the ninth inning.

With Game 2 tied at 3–3, one-out singles by McBride and

Schmidt promised another last-at-bat victory. It looked certain when Smith sliced a base hit to right. McBride, who had hesitated to see if Terry Puhl came up with the catch, took off for home. One step away from third, though, Elia stopped him.

"Lee told me to stop," said McBride. "So I stopped and then he said, 'Go!' You know, by the time he said 'Go!' it was too late."

Two decades later, Elia still believed McBride would have been out. "And the fact that there was only one out kept sticking out in my mind."

The bases were loaded, but the Phillies were as deflated as their fans. Trillo struck out, and Maddox popped out to end the inning. Reprieved, Puhl led off the tenth with a single off Reed. There were Astros at first and second with one out when ~~Todd~~ Jose Cruz's single gave them a 4–3 lead. Cesar Cedeno's infield chopper scored Rafael Landestoy, and Dave Bergman's two-run triple off Saucier made it 7–3.

Philadelphia got a run in the bottom of the inning before Schmidt, on a 3–0 count, flew out to deep right. "I just missed that pitch," said Schmidt.

Facing three games in Houston, nearly everyone in Philadelphia was convinced the Phils had blown another NLCS. They were headed south again, on their way to Astrodoom. Rose cautioned the reporters who gathered at his locker afterward.

"You're the ones who are going to make asses out of yourselves writing Houston has control of this series now," Rose said. "That's really an asinine thing to say."

Asinine or not, it was how people felt who had been watching the Phillies much longer than Rose. On the Broad Street subway, riding back to his northeast Philadelphia home after Game 2, Martin Mandon, 32, interrupted a younger fan who was trying to concoct a hopeful scenario for the Phils.

"It's the last game of the season here, kid," advised Mandon, the voice of experience. "The last game—and we were here to boo it."

While the Phillies dressed and prepared for the 3½-hour flight to Houston, the mood in the city was as laden with gloom as the club's postseason history.

"For the Phillies, October isn't a month," wrote Ray Didinger in the *Daily News*, "it's a padded cell waiting to slam shut on them."

In the NLCS's unforgiving five-game format, there was an enormous difference between a 2–0 lead and 1–1—especially when the next three games were set for the Astrodome.

"If we were going to do it," said Schmidt, "we knew we were going to have to do it down there. They had never been in the play-offs before, so we knew the people would be going nuts."

In Philadelphia, there now was little reason to suspect this 1980 season finally would be the one to bridge the canyon between the dreams of Phillies fans and the reality of Phillies baseball.

"As flies are to little boys," wrote Conlin, "so are the Phillies to the gods; they kill them for sport."

◆ ◆ ◆

Those three weekend games in Houston emotionally drained anyone fortunate enough to have witnessed them.

"The most exciting back-to-back games in baseball history," said Gross.

While the momentum ebbs and flows from dugout to dugout, the tension is ceaseless. Rather than detract from the pressure, the Astrodome only seemed to heighten the dramatic atmosphere, as if all the nervousness and noise were trapped inside and constantly recycled.

"You got the feeling those games could go on and on and on," said McCarver.

From Niekro's first pitch in Game 3 to Ruthven's last in the tenth inning of Game 5, a relentless seriousness colors the play. Things occasionally seem to move in slow motion. And at times, you can see, for the first time maybe, the beauty of such baseball fundamentals as the cutoff play or a drag bunt.

"I don't think there has ever been anything like those games in Houston," said Schmidt. "You were up, then down, then up again. The emotion expended, on both sides, was incredible."

By 1980, the multisport stadium, Astroturf craze the Dome had inspired was at its height. Half the teams in the National League played in big, faceless circular stadiums, and on Astroturf. In fact, that year three of the four play-off teams and, for the first time, both World Series contestants played on the artificial surface.

Texas had never before hosted a major-league postseason game. While Texans loved a spectacle, they didn't quite know what to make of this. Attendance at each of the games was close to 45,000, about 4,000 below the Dome's capacity. Those who came, though, whooped and hollered with all the passion of Friday night football fans. They brought Texas flags and wore the bright orange that was the dominant color in the Astros' garishly striped uniforms.

Had the people of Houston known what they were about to witness, they would have lined up past Galveston for tickets.

Not surprisingly, Game 3, a 1–0 Houston win in 11 innings, showcased pitching. The Phillies nicked Niekro for some early hits, but from the fifth through the tenth got just one, an infield single by Trillo. Houston wasn't much better against Christenson and the Phils bullpen. Through ten innings, the game was scoreless.

Maddox doubled with two outs in the 11th, but Dave Smith struck out Unser. Then to start the Astros' 11th, a hobbling Joe Morgan tripled just beyond McBride's outstretched glove in right-center off McGraw, working in his fourth inning.

Two intentional walks followed before Denny Walling's sacrifice fly to left scored pinch runner Landestoy with the game's first and only run.

The Astros didn't get away from their Game 3 win without paying a price. Centerfielder Cesar Cedeno tripped over first base in the sixth, tore an ankle ligament, and was done for the postseason.

If the Phillies had been disappointed following Game 2, now, on the brink of another crushing conclusion, they were despondent.

"Sometimes you wonder if you're even supposed to get into a World Series," whispered a downcast Bowa. "You wonder if it just isn't in the cards."

"I'd like to be in their shoes over there right now," said Schmidt. "But I still feel we're the best team."

◆　◆　◆

If there were any reason for the Phillies to rally psychologically, it was because Carlton would be going against Vern Ruhle in the next afternoon's must-win Game 4.

But, on three days' rest this time, the left-hander didn't yet seem himself. His slider lacked some of its terrifying bite. His fastballs were sailing high. He walked five and allowed four hits, and when he left with one out in the sixth, Houston was ahead 2–0.

The Astros had nicked Carlton for runs in the fifth and sixth on RBI singles by Art Howe and Landestoy.

One of the moments that provided this series its reputation came in the fourth inning. The game was delayed for 20 minutes as the umpires twice botched a call. Without a run since the tenth inning of Game 2, the Phillies at last were putting together a rally. Runners stood at first and second with no outs when Maddox punched a soft liner back at Ruhle.

The Houston pitcher reached low and gloved it but only, as replays showed, after it had skipped off the turf. The base runners weren't sure what had happened, and they lurched back and forth in confusion. Ruhle threw to first where Howe stepped on the bag and raced to second before a baffled McBride returned.

Home plate umpire Doug Harvey initially got it right, ruling that Maddox was out at first. But he was overruled by base umps Bob Engel and Ed Vargo and eventually signaled that it was a triple play.

With that, a bellowing Green leaped out of the Phillies dugout. Bowa began screaming at Harvey. In the stands, Ruly Carpenter had a bear hug on Owens. "Pope wanted to get at the umpires," said the Phils owner.

As the umpires continued to discuss the play, a frustrated Owens left his seat. In an Astrodome concourse, he bumped into Rollie Hemond, the veteran baseball man.

"I guess that God just doesn't want me to win," Owens told him.

Meanwhile, Schmidt spotted NL president Feeney in his box seat. He headed toward him.

"It's the middle of the ballgame, and I'm in the stands with Chub Feeney," said Schmidt. "I had seen the play clearly, and I'm on my knees begging him to watch the replay."

The umpires huddled, and Harvey, too, conferred with Feeney. Eventually, Harvey reversed himself again, deciding that it was a double play because time had been called before Howe touched second. Both teams protested. More significantly, the Phillies didn't score.

The Phillies' bats were as silent as their dugout. When the eighth inning began, their run of scoreless innings had reached 17. It was all so familiar from postseasons past. Schmidt, Maddox, Luzinski, all of them looked to be pressing, as if anticipating how the next day's headlines might read should they fail. The positive emotions that had bubbled up throughout the last week appeared to have evaporated in the runless, artificial atmosphere of the Dome.

"I honestly couldn't see it ending that way," said Schmidt. "I couldn't see us leaving there without scoring some runs."

Gross and Smith singled off a wearying Ruhle to start the eighth, and the visitors dugout sparked to life. Bowa began pacing and chattering like a magpie. Rose lined an RBI single to center. When Puhl threw to third to try to get Smith, Rose rolled into second. Schmidt smacked a bouncer up the middle that Morgan gloved behind the bag, too late for a play. The game was tied at 2–2.

Trillo's liner to right was caught on a short hop by Jeff Leonard, but Bruce Froemming—the same umpire whose incorrect call at first base on Black Friday allowed the Dodgers to win that 1977 play-off game—ruled it a catch. Schmidt, unsure of what had happened, was doubled off first, but not before Rose scored the go-ahead run.

The umpires again had managed to incense both teams. Schmidt and Green argued that the ball had been trapped. And Houston manager Bill Virdon and his players complained that Rose ought not to have been permitted to score because the double play ended the inning. Incorrectly, and correctly, Harvey informed them that the ball had been caught on the fly but because a forceout was not involved, and Rose had scored before Schmidt was called out, the run stood.

At this stage of the series, the Houston fans expected still more. They shook the Dome in the bottom of the ninth, and Puhl's RBI single, tying the game, rewarded them.

"That," said Green, "was our lowest point."

Bruce Bochy was soon to be just as low and feeling a whole lot worse.

With one out in the tenth, Rose singled off Joe Sambito. One out later, Green sent out Luzinski to pinch-hit for McBride. He smacked a double into the leftfield corner. Cruz played it cleanly and quickly. It didn't appear Rose could possibly score. But he roared around third, not even glancing at Elia, who didn't dare try to halt his hell-bent dash.

"I know Pete Rose," said Morgan, "Pete Rose was never going to stop."

Helmet off, chin cocked for action, he bore down on Bochy as Landestoy's relay throw neared. Distracted by the rumbling Rose, the Astros catcher bobbled the short hop. An instant later, Rose's left forearm clocked him high. Bochy went down. The Phils went up, 4–3.

"We were playing for a lot," Rose recalled. "You do what you can. I knew I wanted to score."

Trillo's double soon made it 5–3. McGraw recorded another scoreless inning. And two innings after it appeared the Phillies' season would soon be over, the series was tied with a single game to play.

"There has never been a game to compare with that one," said McGraw, prematurely as it turned out. "It was like going through an art museum on a motorcycle. You don't remember all the pictures you saw because there were so many and they came so fast."

"It made you wonder," said Owens, "what was going to happen the next night."

◆   ◆   ◆

Somehow it wouldn't have been appropriate if the Phils had won Game 5 in routine fashion. An easy victory wouldn't have been the stake in the heart that their history deserved. Thirty years of pennant-less pain demanded a noteworthy end, one that could bury 23-game losing streaks, Black Friday, and 1964 beneath a mountain of memorable moments.

Given what had preceded it in this NLCS, no one should have been surprised when Game 5 turned out to be one of the best postseason contests ever played.

"I've seen a lot of ballgames, but during that one my knees were shaking like crazy," said Owens. "I couldn't get them to stop."

Curiously, the deciding game's pitching matchup promised nothing of the sort.

Bystrom's brief stretch of glory was nearly at an end that Sunday night. The 6-foot 5-inch 22 year old would never again approach the success he had that September. In five more seasons, his win total never exceeded six.

Bystrom got the word from his manager Saturday night that he, and not a rested Ruthven, would start Game 5. Green and his teammates had confidence in the rookie pitcher. They might have been the only ones who gave him a chance against Ryan.

Ryan threw loose and easy in warm-ups. His fastballs approached 100 MPH in the early innings. And when Houston grabbed a 1–0 lead off Bystrom in the first, it wasn't difficult to envision another shutout win.

In a game filled with turning points, the first occurred in the second inning. With two outs, runners on second and third, and Bystrom on deck, Virdon elected to have Ryan pitch to Boone. The flamethrower unleashed his fastest pitch of the night, 99 MPH, according to the radar guns. Boone slapped it right back up the middle for a two-run single that seemed to suggest Ryan's best might not be enough. The hit gave Philadelphia its first of three leads and left the laconic Astros manager susceptible to eternal second-guessing.

"If a manager had done that in Philadelphia and the Phillies lost," said Carpenter, "he might as well leave town."

Bystrom held on, and the lead held up until the sixth. But the Astros tied it then. For the seventh, Green surprised everyone by turning to Christenson, the sore-armed pitcher who had gone six innings two nights earlier.

"Ron Reed was warming up with me, and he couldn't figure out what I was doing up," recalled Christenson. "When they called for me, I thought he was going to explode."

A Luzinski misplay in left—one that conjured up the Manny Mota disaster of 1977—and a Howe triple helped produce three runs off Christenson and, eventually, Reed. The Astrodome roar ratcheted up to thunder.

"That was the loudest sound I'd ever heard," said Maddox.

At third base, Schmidt placed his hands over his ears.

"I swear to God," said Rose, "I thought the Astrodome would fall down."

Something was wrong with Christenson. Even when his arm was sore, he always competed. This time he appeared uncharacteristically meek on the mound. No one but the pitcher knew it yet but his father, back in Washington, had just suffered an aneurysm and fallen into a coma. He would die a few days after the championship parade. When the inning finally ended, Rose found the pitcher in the dugout and glowered at him.

"I'll never forget Pete Rose," said Christenson, "staring at me, like a Gatling gun sticking out of each eyeball, mowing me down. It went right through me."

The noise continued, and the Astros still led 5–2 when the eighth inning began. The Phillies prospects were dismal. When he had a lead after seven innings, Ryan was 112–3.

In the stands behind the Phillies dugout, Owens glanced at his wife, Marcelle.

"She had these big tears coming down her cheek," said Owens. "I felt like crying, too, but I said, 'What are you crying for? We've got six outs left.'"

Rose yelled the same thing in the team's third-base dugout. He screamed at Bowa, due to lead off. "If you get on base, we're going to win this game!"

Bowa fired right back at him. "Don't worry, I'm going to get on base!"

He did—with a flared single to center. Boone again lined a Ryan fastball back at him. Had the pitcher fielded it cleanly, it would have been a rally-killing double play. Instead, the ball deflected off the pitcher's glove and caromed to third baseman Enos Cabell, whose hurried throw bounced into Howe's glove an instant after the sore-legged Boone crossed the bag.

Now the Phillies dugout sprang to life.

"Everybody was up on the rail. Nobody was sitting down," said Elia, who watched from his third-base coaching box. "It was like an explosion ready to blow one way or the other. It was either going to be tremendous elation or a tremendous down. I'll never forget those looks. Never."

Watching from the on-deck circle as he prepared to pinch-hit, Gross noted how deep Cabell was positioned.

"I told myself if he was there again, I was going to lay one down," said Gross. "I figured Ryan, wanting to get ahead of me, might not throw me his best fastball on the first pitch."

He didn't. And with Cabell back, Gross's backspinning drag bunt was as perfect as Astroturf allows.

"That turf was like asphalt," Ruthven recalled. "You could try that bunt 1,000 times and never get it down that good."

The Phillies had loaded the bases with none out. Rose barked at Ryan and walked on a 3-2 pitch, Ryan's last, following the ball into the catcher's glove in that irritating way of his.

"Pete was out there going, 'You ain't getting me out, Nollie,'" Schmidt recalled. "Can you imagine saying that to Nolan Ryan and then going ahead and proving that you were right? That took a lot of balls on Pete's part. But that was Pete."

Now it was 5–3. Sambito came in and induced pinch hitter Moreland into an RBI grounder to second. It was 5–4.

Up stepped Schmidt, breathing deeply, gripping his bat so firmly that you half expected to see it drip sap.

Virdon called for Forsch. The veteran right-hander struck out the Phils' star looking. Schmidt angrily slapped his bat and, head down, trying to avoid the cameras he knew would be focusing on his disappointment, slumped back to the dugout.

"All over Philadelphia," Rose said later, "you could probably hear the sound of living-room furniture being smashed."

Philadelphians had seen it before. The great balloon of expectation expanding and expanding, until, at precisely the moment it ought to have carried them away, it blew up in their faces. "Surely, that was the crusher, the final blow that would bury this Phillies team with all those other Phillies teams," wrote the Inquirer's Dolson.

Eventually, though, someone had to confront the ghosts and wave them away. Unser might have been sensing the role would be his the previous night. After Game 4, the Phillies' veteran pinch hitter told hitting coach Billy DeMars he wanted to come out early Sunday for extra batting practice.

"I had struck out a couple of times on pitches I normally handle," said Unser. "Billy said, 'Tomorrow might be our last game.' And I said, 'That's why I want to hit.'"

That afternoon, the two shared a taxi from the Shamrock Hilton. DeMars threw him 75 pitches or so and quickly pronounced him ready.

"Now just take that into the game, and you'll be fine," said DeMars.

Unser singled cleanly to center, and the game, incredibly, was tied.

"The biggest hit in my life," said a reprieved Schmidt, "and I didn't get it."

The Phillies bench was as raucous a place as it had ever been. Everyone was on their feet, screaming encouragement, spilling out of the dugout to meet each run scorer. Luzinski, who had changed into a maroon warm-up jersey after he was removed, led the charges. Hopping nonstop, his eyes flaring, his mouth moving, Bowa resembled a six year old with a hot foot.

"It was electric in there," said Bowa.

In a few seconds, the voltage would increase. Trillo laced a ball into the leftfield corner. Two runs scored and the Phils were now in front 7–5, just six outs away from the World Series.

"Manny came to third, and I was so excited," said Elia. "I didn't know what to do. I had enough awareness to know it wouldn't look right if I kissed him. So I bit him. I put teeth marks in his arm."

No one expected the Astros to go down quietly. Sure enough, they jumped on a weary McGraw, who already had worked six innings in the series. RBI singles by Landestoy and

Cruz tied it at 7–7. Even the stoic Virdon couldn't hide a smile as the Astrodome rumbled like a subway express train.

At last, Green, who had been hoping to save the pitcher for Game 1 of the World Series, called on Ruthven in the ninth. He had been upset when the manager passed him over for Bystrom and then for a weary Christenson in the seventh.

"I got mad when they brought Larry in with one day's rest," he said. "I'm thinking 'I've got more rest. Why don't you use me?' But you know, when I walked out to the mound, I felt like I was going to win that game. And that's a feeling I didn't get a whole lot in my career."

He faced six Astros in the next two innings and retired them all. The Phils gave him a lead to hold in the tenth.

Unser began the pennant-winning rally with a tough-hop double over Bergman's head at first. He moved to third on Trillo's long fly ball to center. Now it was Maddox.

"I went up there thinking first pitch fastball," said Maddox.

What Maddox didn't say is that he *always* went to home plate looking for a first pitch fastball. Frank LaCorte knew that too, but, incredibly, gave him one right down the chute anyway.

Maddox ripped it into center, just in front of a charging Puhl. Unser scored easily, and the Phillies led 8–7. Three outs later, when Maddox squeezed Cabell's line drive to right-center, it was over.

Trillo, who hit .450 (9-for-20) and helped save Game 5 with another brilliant relay throw, was named the series MVP. Boone, both his knees already aching, now had a badly bruised left foot after getting spiked by Cabell on a play at the plate.

At the final out, Owens leaped out of his seat to join Green for a whirling hug near home plate. Phillies players hoisted Maddox onto their shoulders and paraded him to the clubhouse. Two of the season's chief antagonists were afloat in this dizzying joy.

So was everyone else. The Phillies were going back to the World Series. And oddly for a franchise that hadn't been there in 30 years, the players sensed the real battle was over. They were going to beat the Kansas City Royals.

"The script was in," Boone said. "We win. We knew we had to go through a lot to get here. But we knew what the ending was."

Chapter 9

From Hemorrhoids to Heaven

And the last shall be first.

MATTHEW 19:30

Anyone who expected the city's first World Series in 30 years to be a Philly Feel-Good Festival didn't know Philadelphia. They probably couldn't even distinguish a cheesesteak from cheesecake.

Game 1 was still a day away when the Phillies' fans resumed their feud with the team, and a local TV commentator greeted the visitors—the "Canker City Boils," he called the Kansas City Royals—by urging them to get out of town. Then, when the Series began, the level of decorum dipped even further when hemorrhoids threatened to obscure the games themselves.

It all started on Monday afternoon with the city still palpitating from Game 5 of the NLCS.

As soon as that stirring Phillies win had concluded in Houston, fans began gathering at International Airport, built in the Delaware River marshes, just a few miles away from Veterans Stadium. By the time the team's United charter landed there the following day, more than 5,000 were waiting.

The crowd included the usual assortment—longtime fans who sensed the historical significance, newly created enthusiasts, curious onlookers, and those seeking an excuse to party. And this being Philadelphia, one whimsical greeter even carried a sign that referred to the 30-year gap between Phillies pennants and the 76ers' notoriously ill-chosen "We Owe You One" slogan: "You owe us 30!" it read.

Several players, Boone, Rose, Trillo, McGraw, Unser, walked to a makeshift podium and briefly addressed the gathering. Green, Owens, and Carpenter greeted fans, too. The other 18 players, though, went immediately to a waiting bus.

Some of the fans, many of whom had waited all night, were disturbed. So, too, were several local newspaper columnists. The next day's news rang with condemnations of the Phillies' snub. As a result, for what must have been one of the few times in history, a World Series dawned with criticism being directed at the home team.

Bowa tried to explain that team officials had identified the Game 5 heroes and asked them to speak. But Maddox and Ruthven had as big a role as anyone in the victory, and they were on the bus with Schmidt, Luzinski, Carlton, McBride, and the others.

"No one asked us to speak," said Bowa. "The team told us to go right to the bus."

◆ ◆ ◆

Just before midnight on Sunday night, a chartered airplane filled with the Kansas City Royals taxied down a runway at Newark International Airport. The Royals had clinched their first American League pennant Friday night at Yankee Stadium, but stayed in Manhattan until they learned if they'd be going to Houston or Philadelphia for the World Series.

They watched the final innings of Game 5 in an airport lounge before filing onto the plane for the short hop to Philly. In a window seat near the front of the aircraft, George Brett, whose upper-deck home run off Goose Gossage had clinched the three-game sweep, squirmed uncomfortably.

Hemorrhoids.

He had first noticed the pain during Game 3 of the ALCS. But in all the celebration that followed Kansas City's historic victory, Brett had briefly forgotten about his backside blues. The champagne and Italian food hadn't helped any. When, on Saturday, he went shopping with a few teammates, it felt like his pants were on fire.

Great, Brett must have felt, I finally get to a World Series and I've got a problem that's not only physically distressing but embarrassing. What a pain in the— He stopped himself. No sense making bad jokes. The hundreds of wisecracking sportswriters waiting in Philly would take care of that once they learned of his ailment . . . *if* they learned of his ailment.

◆ ◆ ◆

In the hours before Game 1, reporters and broadcasters swarmed across the stretch of foul territory between Veterans Stadium's two dugouts. They talked among themselves, and when a player or coach ventured onto the field, one or two would pull him aside. Very soon, the number of microphones and notebooks would expand 20-fold.

Among the media masses searching for an angle, word spread quickly about the Phillies. Carlton didn't talk. Bowa hadn't been talking. Maddox sometimes didn't talk. This team and its manager—"the fucking Gestapo" Luzinski had called him—fought all year. Players ripped the fans. Fans booed them in September.

That was more than enough. Soon the Philadelphia Phillies would be portrayed, coast to coast, and not entirely inaccurately, as baseball's bad guys. "Those Malevolent Phillies," read the headline on a *Newsweek* story.

"(Three or four Philadelphia writers) told the national media during the play-offs and World Series that we weren't cooperative," Boone said in *The Team That Wouldn't Die.* "I think this team was as cooperative as any team I've ever been around. We spent hours upon hours talking, explaining each aspect of the games, whatever. Still we got a bad rap. So, I think what finally happened was the players no longer tried to live down a reputation—they tried to live up to it.

"The feeling you get, I guess, is 'If I'm going to get ripped for doing this, I might as well be as uncooperative as possible. Take the easy road.' That's where the players on this team are coming from."

Somehow McGraw and *Inquirer* columnist Bill Lyon managed to find some isolation in a corner of the Phillies dugout before Game 1. The Phillies reliever informed the writer that what he was about to tell him couldn't be used until the Series had ended. McGraw whispered that there was no way the Phillies could lose.

"What this team did was tap a whole new resource," said McGraw. "Instead of being emotionally drained, we are emotionally renewed. We learned a lot about ourselves in Montreal and Houston. Those guys don't stand a chance. This team has just discovered it's got something it never knew it had."

◆ ◆ ◆

There was more than enough World Series hype and hoopla on Monday and Tuesday to satisfy the starved locals.

Sports and entertainment celebrities were showing up at

Bookbinder's and Le Bec Fin, the hot new French restaurant chef Georges Perrier had opened on Walnut Street.

The Main Line estates emptied for the invitation-only parties in downtown hotel ballrooms and the great halls of museums.

Sportswriters and broadcasters from around the country, scouts and baseball officials, visitors from Kansas City, strolled Philadelphia's narrow downtown streets.

Old-timers said the city hadn't experienced any excitement like this since the Democrats and Republicans both held their conventions there during the summer of 1948.

Some people pointed out that a few of the post–World War II Army–Navy games had electrified Center City, too. And President Wilson came to town for the 1915 World Series between the Phillies and Red Sox. But, heck, Baker Bowl held less than 20,000 people, and you didn't have the nonstop information blitz that TV and radio now created.

When the Whiz Kids and Yankees met in 1950, there was a buzz in town to be sure. But aside from the big crowds that greeted the Phils at the railway station, the gatherings outside Connie Mack before Games 1 and 2, and a few extra stories in the newspapers, there weren't many physical manifestations of the event.

This time, thanks to television, the whole city had experienced the unstoppable drama of the NLCS. Everyone had World Series fever, even if Philadelphia's baseball temperature seemed to have dropped a little since Sunday night.

It was unrealistic to expect that the Phillies and their fans could again climb the same emotional heights they had reached in the deliciously desperate NLCS.

"I think that after that, everyone was mentally and physically tired," said Bowa. "The World Series was still the World Series, but it couldn't help but be a little bit of a letdown."

Game 1 would be the first Phillies game in more than two weeks—save the meaningless last-day contest in Montreal—that didn't possess a compelling urgency.

"We've been through a nice kind of hell the last ten days," said Green. "It's nice to have a game where your backs aren't up against the wall."

The Phils manager inadvertently heightened the sense that the World Series could be anticlimactic when he revealed that rookie Bob Walk, who had not even thrown a pitch in the Houston series, would start Game 1. The Phillies' other tired and achy starters needed rest after the NLCS.

Walk would be the first rookie since Brooklyn's Joe Black in 1952 to start a Series opener.

"My first reaction," said Walk, "was 'Why would he start me?'"

The answer was simple. There was no one else.

"What the hell choice did I have?" said Green. "But we knew Bobby would give us a good effort. He did win 11 games for us that year."

Just 23, Walk was an unlikely figure for the spotlight. He still had an adolescent's complexion and was so naturally prone to sloppiness that he reminded some teammates of Pigpen, the perpetually dirty "Peanuts" character.

The Phillies called him "Whirlybird" because he was as goofy as a left-hander. He had walked to the plate on one occasion this year without a bat. After being knocked out of a start, Walk drove home, then returned for the postgame interviews. Another time, getting treated in the trainer's room one night, he was watching a game on TV. "What's this?" he asked, "'This Week in Baseball'?" No, he was told, this was a Phillies game that, by the way, was being played just outside.

As a 19 year old, Walk's first pitch to a major-leaguer had gotten him arrested at Dodgers Stadium. Sitting with friends in the bleachers, Walk had tossed a tennis ball at Houston center-fielder Cesar Cedeno.

"I was drunk," he explained.

Just one year earlier Walk had been pumping gas for $3.75 an hour in his native Newhall, California. He won 11 games in 1980, but it wasn't easy. On August 1, he was 8–1 and seemingly headed for Rookie of the Year honors. But he had gone 3–6 since and shaken his manager's confidence in him.

No pitcher ought to be named Walk, particularly one with control problems. The newspapers had a field day when he issued 15 bases-on-balls in his first 26⅓ innings after joining the team in May.

"When the Phillies called me up, the enormity of the whole thing got to me," he said.

He had settled down to become a capable starter but remained too inconsistent for his manager's taste. Still, the kid had guts.

"He'll give us everything he's got," predicted Green.

He would need it against the formidable Royals.

Leadoff hitter Willie Wilson led the AL in runs (133), hits (230), and triples (15) and was second to Oakland's Rickey Henderson in stolen bases with 79. Brett led in batting average (.390), on-base percentage (.461), and slugging percentage (.664). He hit 24 homers and was second in RBIs with 118. Hal McRae hit .297 with 14 homers and 83 RBIs. Willie Mays Aikens's numbers were .278, 20, and 98.

Most believed the Royals, better rested and with a deeper rotation, would win, probably in six games. Asked what his telecasts hoped to focus on during the Series, NBC producer George Finkel provided a summary of the consensus thinking, leaving one to wonder how the flawed Phillies had made it this far.

"We're looking at the excellence of George Brett and the sheer velocity of Willie Wilson," said Finkel.

What about the Phillies?

"We're looking at the question mark of Mike Schmidt during the play-offs, at Tug McGraw proving he's only human with a tired arm, and at, other than Steve Carlton, the questionable Phillies pitching staff."

If he had added, "And then we'll be examining their bank statements," Philadelphians would not have been shocked.

Just how "questionable" the Phils staff was became evident at 8:14 P.M. on Tuesday night, when, just seconds after Whiz Kids manager Eddie Sawyer threw out the first ball, Walk took the mound in front of a record crowd of 65,791.

If you listened closely in those packed stands, you heard the same comment over and over. "Thirty years we wait for a World Series and Bob Walk is the best we can do?"

Standing in the on-deck circle was Wilson. The K.C. lead-off hitter had a breathtaking regular season. But he had holes. He hardly ever walked (just 28 times in 705 at bats), and Philadelphia scouts believed you could sometimes tie him up with high fastballs.

That wasn't the case with the rest of the Royals. Phillies scout Hugh Alexander had warned that hitter-friendly Veterans Stadium would turn some of Kansas City's doubles hitters into home-run sluggers.

"They proved that real quick," said Bowa.

Amos Otis belted a two-run homer off Walk in the second and Aikens, on his 26th birthday, did the same in the third. The Phillies trailed 4–0, and a huge gathering primed to explode sat on its hands. Yet, as if even on this historic night they were reluctant to get out of practice, fans occasionally booed Luzinski, Maddox, and Bowa.

No one relied on the emotional juice a noisy crowd provided more than Bowa. That's why he loved playing in Philadelphia. Even as he walked to the plate with one out in the Phils third, he could hear boos. A little more than two weeks earlier he had called them the "worst fucking fans in the world!"

"The World Series," he chuckled to himself, "and they're booing me."

So when he singled for his team's first hit, he decided to try to ignite them a little more.

Despite the four-run deficit, Bowa defied baseball wisdom and, on a 1–1 pitch, took off for second. Even though Kansas City starter Dennis Leonard hadn't been paying much attention, Bowa barely beat Darrell Porter's throw.

"I knew if I was out I might as well keep running," said Bowa of his risky play.

As he had hoped, the fans' volume increased to ear-splitting levels and stayed there the rest of the Series. And as Bowa stood at second base, applauding his success, his tired teammates stirred.

Boone followed with an RBI double to left, and the Phillies were on the scoreboard. Smith singled and, typically for a player whose nickname was "Skates," tripped rounding first. The throw had come to third, but Brett threw back to first. Smith was out after a rundown, but Brett's throw had allowed Boone to score.

"Blame 65,000 screaming fans for that," said Jim Frey. "You couldn't hear anything tonight."

There were two outs when Rose deliberately allowed himself to be hit on the calf by a pitch.

"He always does that crap," said an agitated Leonard later. "In fact, he might even have stuck his leg out."

"I do remember I didn't try real hard to avoid it," said Rose. "But we needed to get something going."

Clearly unnerved now, Leonard walked Schmidt. That brought up McBride. Over the weekend in Houston, the outfielder had had a tough time on and off the field. He hadn't hit well and then, with his team fighting for its life, he told ABC's Howard Cosell during a pregame interview that he might not want to play for Green again.

On Monday, he and several teammates skipped optional batting practice. But McBride arrived early Tuesday for extra BP with DeMars.

"About the fifth pitch, I started feeling better," he said.

He turned on a Leonard fastball, sending it screaming into the backdrop in rightfield. The three-run homer gave the Phils a 5–4 lead, and the standing, shouting spectators demanded a curtain call from McBride.

The Phils added single runs in the next two innings and, despite Aikens's second two-run homer in the eighth, held on. McGraw, as usual, finished up with two scoreless, one-hit innings.

The Phillies now not only had their starting pitching back on track but had ended a 65-year winless stretch in World Series games. That was a significant historical milepost given the way things worked in Philly.

All through the final weeks, the Phillies had been reminded about the collapse of 1964. They ended that annoying talk in Montreal.

Then, when they lost Games 2 and 3 of the NLCS, they were confronted with their three previous NLCS disappointments. That faded the moment they eliminated Houston.

But between then and the start of the Series, all anyone talked about, it seemed, was the fact that their last—and only—World Series win had come on October 8, 1915.

"You play here," said Bowa, "you live with ghosts."

◆ ◆ ◆

Brett's discomfort had worsened during Game 1. He regretted eating sausage and peppers at the row home of Al and Evelyn Bianchini, Philadelphia fans who lived near the stadium and who had befriended his brother Ken when the Royals pitcher was with the Phillies a few years earlier.

He had managed to keep news of his ailment inside the clubhouse, though a persistent reporter, watching him limp back to his locker 90 minutes after Game 1, had asked him if were hurting.

"No," Brett lied.

By early the next morning, he couldn't stand it anymore. Brett summoned trainer Mickey Cobb to his room in the half-finished Franklin Plaza. The trainer arranged a visit to a nearby proctologist, Dr. Benjamin Haskell. Haskell prescribed rest and treatment with a salve.

Word had leaked out by then and reporters intercepted Brett as, walking in a gingerly, bow-legged manner, he returned to the hotel.

"I'll play tonight," he predicted.

He did, collecting two singles and a walk before telling Frey in the sixth inning that he could no longer continue. The Phillies then led the Series 2–1, and Brett felt responsible. On another night, he said, he would have had at least one of the two base hits that whizzed past him in the Phillies' fifth.

Carlton was—relatively speaking—laboring again. He would throw 159 pitches in eight innings on a chilly South Philadelphia night, allowing ten hits and six walks while striking out ten.

Green blamed his ace's troubles on slick baseballs. New balls, bearing Commissioner Bowie Kuhn's name instead of the league presidents', had been ordered for the Series.

"They were as slick as any I've ever seen," said Green. "Boonie told me they were as slick as ice."

Leonard, who won 20 games in the regular season, had mentioned the same problem after Game 1, saying he never could get command of his breaking ball.

Still, it was 0–0 before Trillo's sacrifice fly and Bowa's RBI single scored a pair of Philadelphia runs in the fifth. K.C. got its first three runners on in the sixth, but scored just once—Otis coming home on Trillo's throwing error—as Cardenal fanned and White bounced into a double play.

As had happened in the Houston series, the Royals put the Phils in a late-inning hole, this time scoring three times in the seventh for a 4–2 lead.

Three Carlton walks filled the bases with one out. Otis doubled past a diving Schmidt to score two, and John Wathan's sacrifice fly made it 4–2. Though left-handed starter Larry Gura had permitted just four hits, Frey wanted Dan Quisenberry to start the seventh.

The mustachioed, poetry-writing, submarining right-hander had tied Gossage for the AL lead with 33 saves in his breakout season. He checked the Phils in the seventh, and on the home team's bench, Green yelled the same words he had been using through a month's worth of rallies.

"Hey bench, let's get things going!"

Boone started it off with a walk. Unser pinch-hit for Smith and laced a run-scoring double into the left-centerfield gap. Rose's right-side grounder pushed Unser to third, from where he scored on McBride's game-tying single, bounced over a drawn-in infield.

Heeding some advice from his father, Schmidt swung at Quisenberry's first pitch, doubling home McBride.

"I have a tendency to take a look at a guy's first pitch most of the time, to check out his velocity, his breaking ball, and see how he's trying to set me up," Schmidt said.

Moreland, the DH since Luzinski was suffering from an intestinal ailment, scored him with a single.

Unser's hit had turned another game around. After coming off the bench to spark Sunday's remarkable comeback at the Astrodome, the 35-year-old reserve outfielder now had three enormous two-base hits in three consecutive at bats.

Talking about his quiet teammate, Bowa directed some rare praise toward his manager—and, by extension, criticism toward Ozark.

"This team used to be eight regulars, four starting pitchers, and a reliever," he said. "Dallas has utilized 25 players. When the late innings come along, we have guys who know they'll contribute."

Green at last gave McGraw a night off, and Reed struck out a pair of Royals to record the save. The Phillies were going to Kansas City with a 2–0 lead, one that seemed even more formidable given the two comebacks and the questions—the ifs, ands, and *butts*—about Brett's ability to perform.

"You've got to wonder what we've got to do to beat the Phillies," said Wilson.

◆ ◆ ◆

Brett got some relief—from the pain if not the bad jokes—on the flight home, stretching out over three seats.

He was the only Royal who had much room on the plane. Most Royals officials and their wives had traveled to Philadelphia for the Series. They came home on the charter. So instead of 40 or 50 people rattling around a plane, there were 140.

Basic Agreement guidelines stipulated that those players who couldn't be accommodated in first class must have an empty seat next to them. In other words, three seats for every two players. That wasn't the case this time, and a lot of the Royals players were upset.

If there were still any fans in America who didn't yet consider baseball players to be spoiled and pampered, the Royals did their best to change their minds. Pete LaCock, their player representative, filed a grievance over the seating accommodations.

Once the flight arrived in Kansas City, Brett took a cab to St. Luke's Hospital. Early the next morning, an off day, he had the hemorrhoids lanced.

Improvement came quickly. By the time Game 3 began, Brett was joking that the worst was behind him and that he had volunteered to be used as the lineup's Preparation DH.

"It's easier to be lighthearted about it now that I'm not in so much pain," he said.

He immediately—and thankfully—made hemorrhoids a nonissue by homering off Ruthven in the first inning, giving the Royals a 1–0 lead and touching off an explosion of glee among the 42,380 Royals Stadium fans at the first World Series game ever in that city.

Before the game, Frey had surprised a lot of his players by calling a team meeting. The crusty manager was profane and funny, and the Royals left the clubhouse considerably looser.

"I felt the players were a little tight in Philadelphia," he explained. "The crowds and the World Series atmosphere seemed to intimidate them. I told them that I thought they were the best team in America . . . to go have some fun."

The Phillies tied Game 3 at 1–1 in the second on Trillo's bases-loaded ground ball to pitcher Rich Gale. K.C. re-took one-run advantages in the fourth and seventh, only to see Philadelphia even the score an inning later in each case.

The red-hot Aikens, who had asked the media to drop the "Mays" from his name, tripled in the fourth and came home on McRae's single.

Schmidt, who had flied out with the bases loaded in the second, clubbed a home run to left that tied it in the fifth. Otis homered in the seventh, and Rose's RBI single in the eighth made it 3–3—the fifth straight game in which the Phils had rallied to tie or take the lead after the seventh inning.

The Phils looked poised to jump ahead in the tenth. With one out, Boone on second and Rose at first, Schmidt smashed a Quisenberry pitch the other way. Second baseman White made a tough stop of the short hop and triggered a threat-killing double play.

McGraw entered in the tenth. The left-hander might have had Game 2 off, but he had thrown an incredible 15⅔ pressure-jammed innings between the October 2 win over Chicago and Game 1 of the World Series. No wonder more and more of the fastballs he named were either "Peggy Lees" ("Is That All There Is?") or "John Jamesons" ("Just like I drink my Irish whiskey. Straight.").

U. L. Washington, a toothpick dangling from his mouth, singled on the reliever's first pitch. Wilson tried to sacrifice him to second, but McGraw walked him on four pitches. White missed a bunt attempt, but Washington kept running. Boone threw him out, and a huge national TV audience saw Frey scowl in the dugout. So much for having fun.

"The only one to blame," said Frey, "is the base runner."

And that wasn't even the inning's worst base running blunder. White eventually struck out, and with Brett, who was 5-for-10 in the World Series at that point and arguably baseball's best hitter, at bat, Wilson took off for second.

Boone had called for a pitchout—leading several K.C. players to suggest later that the Phils had stolen their signs—but he bounced a throw to second. While Wilson was successful, he had forced the Phils to walk Brett, further irritating his manager.

"No way he had the steal sign," said Frey. "He went on his own and ended up taking the bat out of Brett's hands."

Aikens muted the potential controversy, though, lining a 2–1 pitch over Maddox's head in left-center. The Royals had their first World Series win, 4–3.

The somber-faced first baseman had been born in October of 1954, just after Mays' Giants had defeated Cleveland in the World Series. The doctor in the delivery room, a baseball fan, added the "Mays" when he heard that the Aikens's baby's first name would be Willie.

"I prefer just 'Willie,'" said Aikens, whose pleas weren't aided by the fact that he also wore Mays's No. 24. "Nobody uses Hal McRae's middle name. Or George Brett's."

A hot hitter by any other name, however, remains a hot hitter. Aikens kept up his barrage in Game 4, homering off a completely ineffective Christenson in the first and Dickie Noles in the second.

"You sure this isn't really Willie Mays?" asked Rose.

◆ ◆ ◆

Luzinksi hadn't played in Game 3, and he wasn't in Green's lineup for Game 4 either. That meant three straight games on the bench. The designated-hitter rule then was employed in alternating years and the 1980 Series used it.

Luzinski seemed like the ideal DH. But Moreland filled that role in Game 3 while Smith played left. Smith then DH'd in Game 4 while Green gave the left-handed-hitting Unser a start against Leonard.

Luzinski, who had missed Game 2 with the flu, stewed. The speculation on his benching began. Maybe he was still sick. Maybe Green was punishing him for his "Gestapo" comment. The manager denied it all.

"I love Greg Luzinski," he said. "And I'd love to play him. But I'm not the one who hit .228."

Whatever the reason, Luzinski was back in leftfield for Game 5.

In the first inning of Game 4, Wilson singled. Christenson's wild pickoff throw sent him to third. He held there on White's fly ball to shallow right and scored on Brett's triple. Aikens then hit his third home run, and the Royals led 3–0.

McRae slapped a hit up the middle, and when Maddox was slow to throw back, stretched it into a double.

"I had noticed how the Philadelphia outfielders tended to throw lollipops back to the infield," said McRae.

Otis doubled off the wall in right, and it was 4–0.

"After I warmed up and went back to the dugout," Christenson recalled, "I heard Dallas ask (pitching coach) Herm Starrette, 'What's he got?' Herm said, 'He ain't got shit.' I had nothing. I was trying to knock down Aikens, and he hit a home run."

That was all for Christenson. Green called on Noles.

The Phillies got a run back in the second, but in the bottom of the inning Aikens crushed a 2–1 pitch into the waterfall beyond the centerfield wall. This time, as he had after his first one in Game 1, the Royals cleanup hitter took time to stand and watch his blast.

"I gave that second one a long look," he said.

The fiery Noles seethed on the mound. With Brett and Aikens enjoying batting practice against his staff, Green knew it was time for something else.

"We had to start pitching differently," he said.

Christenson had wanted to knock down Aikens. Noles was planning to do the same to the Royals' red-hot first baseman. But when he got ahead of Brett 0–2, the plot changed. Boone called for a knockdown now. Noles wasn't sure if he wanted to drill the Kansas City star or just move him back.

"I got two fastballs right by him," said Noles. "He fouled both of them off, real late. On the second fastball he just stood out over the plate for a long time. (He) kind of looked like, 'How did I miss it?' I'm standing on the mound thinking, 'I know how you missed it. I threw the ball by you.' I wasn't sure whether to hit him or knock him down," said Noles. "That's why the pitch ended up where it did."

The searing fastball headed directly for Brett's neck. He flopped back desperately, landing, as Rose would say, "right on his hemorrhoids."

Frey flew out of the dugout toward home-plate umpire Don Denkinger.

"Stop it right now! Stop it right now!" he screamed. The manager yelled something toward Noles, who replied angrily. Rose joined the gathering turmoil near the mound, telling Frey to get back in the dugout.

"He was yelling at our pitcher," said Rose. "I had never seen that before. Brett was the guy who could have been screaming, and he wasn't saying a word."

Rose stopped to talk with Noles before he returned to first base.

"Pitch your game," he told him. "You want to knock somebody else down, go ahead."

Noles struck out Brett. And Aikens.

The Royals wouldn't score again—in fact, they would score just four more runs in the final two and a half games of the

Series—but the Phils could manage just lone runs in the seventh and eighth off Leonard and Quisenberry.

With the 5–3 victory, the Royals had tied the Series at 2–2, and the pivotal fifth game would be played on their home field in less than 24 hours.

"I just didn't like the way we went about our work in the first couple innings," said Green. "They were taking extra bases and using their running game pretty much as they wanted. They were swinging the bats as they wanted. Their pitcher didn't have the great stuff, but we didn't get to him."

That was as critical as Green had been in the postseason. Not surprisingly, his players didn't allow him a free pass.

"That's ridiculous," said Schmidt. "That's just second-guessing. If they don't score four runs, he never says that, right? And what did anybody have to do with that except the pitcher and the catcher?"

The Phillies now had played a remarkable 13 consecutive games decided by one or two runs.

"Right now, I just want to get out of here with a win on Sunday," said Schmidt. "Somebody asked me if we had run out of miracles. Everybody keeps talking about luck and miracles and heart and character, but we've got talent, too."

◆ ◆ ◆

One way or another, the Phillies were going to need a big victory at home in Game 6, so Green gave Carlton an extra day's rest and revealed that Bystrom would again be pitching a crucial Game 5.

The Royals had been very patient with Carlton's devastating slider, laying off it time and time again and allowing it to break out of the strike zone, something NL hitters had difficulty doing. Green knew his ace would need to rely on his fastball against them, and he figured an extra day might add some velocity.

"I knew it was a gamble to throw a kid out there in Game 5," said Green. "But I knew I would have Lefty and Ruthven back to back. If they beat us, they were going to have beat our best."

Game 5 was scoreless when, with one out in the fourth, McBride nubbed a slow roller between Gura and first base. The pitcher hurriedly fielded it and tossed. Aikens caught the ball but never could find first with his feet. McBride was safe on his error.

Schmidt then slammed a 2–2 Gura pitch over the 410-foot sign in straightaway center and the Phillies were in front 2–0.

The Royals got a run back in the fifth. Washington and Wilson singled and were advanced by White's sacrifice bunt. Brett's infield grounder sent Washington home. They went ahead 3–2 in the sixth on Otis's third homer of the Series and, after Reed replaced Bystrom, Washington's sacrifice fly to right.

Once again, a perfect relay from McBride to Trillo to Boone saved Philadelphia.

"Sometime during the season, they had messed up a relay," said Green of McBride and Trillo. "So they went out there early one day and practiced about 75 of them."

With Porter on first in the sixth, Wilson doubled off the wall in right. McBride took the ricochet cleanly and found Trillo. The second baseman's one-hop BB to Boone got Porter.

"If Trillo doesn't make that play, they could have gone on to a big inning and taken us right out of the game," said Rose.

If the relay throw had become a familiar staple of the Phillies' postseason, so had the elements that followed—good fortune, a late-inning rally, a clutch Unser double, and another hair-raising McGraw save.

"You kept saying to yourself, 'Haven't we seen this before?'" said Schmidt. "We kept doing the things we needed to do to win over and over."

Three outs from being swept in K.C., Schmidt led off the ninth. Brett asked Frey if he wanted him to play in for a possible bunt. The Phillies third baseman had bunted, just foul, in the eighth inning of Game 3, and the Royals knew their opponents were desperate for a base runner.

"Don't give it to him," Frey told Brett.

Brett positioned himself even with the bag. Had he been a step or two back, he would have gloved the line-drive single that Schmidt ripped off his glove.

"I had no intention of bunting in that situation," said Schmidt. "As a leadoff hitter, I was just trying to drive the ball some place. I did notice that Brett was playing me in, though."

Unser, who had started in left, doubled just inside Aikens, a ball that a better fielding first baseman than Aikens might have caught. Schmidt raced home, and the score was even.

"The ball bounced just over Aikens's glove by maybe two or three inches," said Unser. "I hit the ball probably as good as I can hit a ball. I don't know what he could have done on that ball."

Moreland sacrificed Unser to third, but Maddox grounded out.

With two outs, Trillo lined an 0–2 Quisenberry pitch right back at him. It bounced away from the pitcher and toward third. Brett raced in, scooped it up, and fired, but Trillo was safe and Unser had scored the go-ahead run.

McGraw had been out drinking the previous night, and he wouldn't have been entirely unhappy with a day off. When the bullpen phone rang in the sixth inning, and coach Mike Ryan told him to get ready, his eyes were bloodshot and his head was pounding. His arm felt worse.

He came in for the seventh and had little trouble until the ninth when he walked White to begin the inning. He got a huge lift when, for a second time, he struck out Brett on a fastball on the outside corner.

"That was one of the biggest thrills of my career," said McGraw. "He's probably the greatest hitter in baseball right now. One of the things I thought of (with two strikes) was maybe coming on him real good inside—you know, pitch him from the Dickie Noles School of Baseball. But I thought Mr. Frey might get all excited."

McGraw walked Aikens before McRae ripped a breaking ball deep to left. The crowd jumped to its feet anticipating a game-winning homer. But this was 1980, not 1950. The ball hooked into the seats, just to the left of the foul pole and, before getting McRae to bounce out, McGraw playfully patted his heart.

"I was thinking, I can't take many more of these tense games," said McGraw.

The Phils closer was careful with Otis, walking him on four pitches (his fifth in three innings) to load the bases. Up stepped pinch hitter Cardenal, a Phillie in 1978 and 1979.

"Jose is dangerous with men on base, but because I knew him from when he was with the Cubs and with us, I felt fairly comfortable pitching to him," said McGraw.

The count went to 1–2. Cardenal fouled off a pair of pitches. On one of those foul balls, his bat slipped and landed near the mound. Cardenal asked him to return it, and the pitcher told him to come and get it. They exchanged angry words, and when Cardenal came to reclaim it, McGraw stuck the bat in his gut.

"He said something to me in Spanish that you wouldn't hear in church," recalled McGraw, "so when I handed the bat back, I jabbed him in the stomach."

McGraw then struck him out with a fastball that sailed inside, the pitch he called "Cutty Sark."

The three games in Kansas City complete, someone asked Bowa, by now a noted fan expert, how these Midwestern spectators compared to Philadelphians.

"They don't know how to be mean here," he said. "They know how to be mean in Philly."

No one said so publicly, but returning home, with a rested Carlton on the mound and a 3–2 lead, the Phillies felt that they were going to win, that the Series was over when they left Kansas City that Sunday night.

"I told my wife, 'It's over,'" recalled Bowa. "We had Lefty on the mound, and you could just feel it in the city."

◆ ◆ ◆

On the morning of October 21, McGraw left his home near suburban Media and drove the short distance to Schmidt's sprawling brick house along Springton Lake. That was their pregame routine. Pick him up at 3, stop for a milkshake, and drive to the Vet.

The reliever had sensed victory since Game 1. Now, as he, Schmidt, and the pitcher's older brother Frank, an ex-Phillies minor-leaguer, headed down Interstate 95 to the ballpark, the normally emotionally cautious Schmidt shared his optimism. He even had a request for the Phillies closer.

Figuring McGraw would be on the mound at the end of a Game 6 victory, Schmidt asked him to wait after he had recorded the final out.

"I had been seeing those pictures all my life," Schmidt said. "Guys leaping into each other's arms at the end of a World Series. Now here I was with a chance to be that guy. So I told Tug to hold up and I'd come over and jump on him."

That was fine with McGraw. He just hoped his left arm held up that long. For some time now, it ached so much that he had been popping two or three Tylenol in the afternoon and two or three more in the fourth inning.

"If it wasn't for the pills," McGraw said, "I wouldn't have made it through the last month."

The excitement that had been building for the last three and a half weeks engulfed the city that day. The morning and afternoon passed in a sort of surreal haze. These were Philadelphians and yet, they too, seemed convinced a Game 6 loss was impossible.

Fans tried to imagine what form the victory celebration might take. Riots? Parades? Clogged streets? Bar fights?

Clusters of them made plans to meet after the game in neighborhood taverns, Center City restaurants, at busy intersections throughout the area.

Carpenter, like his players, wondered what form the revelry might take.

"Hell, when they tore old Connie Mack Stadium up," the owner said, "I saw guys in three-piece suits carrying toilets out of the men's room."

An upbeat, wildly anticipatory air filled Veterans Stadium. So did 65,839 spectators, a record for a baseball game in Pennsylvania. Like the players, these people wanted badly for it to end. The thought of a Game 7 and its potential for more history-making disappointment was too traumatic to envision. After 14 straight games decided by one or two runs, everyone deserved a break.

Milling among them were hundreds of riot-helmeted Philadelphia policeman. City officials, recalling the riotous behavior of New Yorkers after the Mets' championship in 1969 and Yankees' ALCS triumph in 1976, had taken extraordinary precautions.

"We wanted to show we were in control," explained police commissioner Morton Solomon.

What the fans couldn't see were the dozen mounted policemen and an equal number of police dogs in the runway beneath the stadium. Solomon's plan was for the horses to cross the field in the seventh inning, letting any potential rowdies know what awaited them at game's end.

"The whole idea," said Solomon, "was for there to be a show of force rather than a utilization of force."

Carlton and Gale were in control early, and it was 0–0 as Boone stepped to home plate to start the Phillies' third. He walked. Smith, back in left as Luzinski DH'd, grounded to White, who flipped to Washington. The shortstop cheated, as shortstops hurrying to make a double play often do, and his foot scraped past the bag.

But this could be a historic night and second-base ump Bill Kunkel apparently decided a "phantom" tag wasn't good enough for such an occasion. He signaled Boone safe, Smith beat the return throw, and the Phillies had a rally.

The bases were loaded after Rose's bunt hit, between Gale and Brett.

Schmidt then laced a fastball into right field, and the din must have shaken Camden. Boone scored. Smith, who really did appear to play on roller skates, stumbled rounding third. The noise was so great, however, that the Royals never noticed. He popped off the turf and sprinted home. The Phillies led 2–0.

Smith's speed, an underrated factor in the Phillies' September play, next turned a fifth-inning leadoff hit to center into a double. Rose's fly ball to Otis sent him to third. When Renie Martin walked Schmidt, Frey called for Paul Splittorf.

McBride's dribbler to short scored Smith, and it was 3–0.

After Bowa's sixth-inning double and Boone's single to center, their lead was 4–0.

Carlton had allowed just three singles in seven innings. But when Wathan walked and Cardenal singled to start the eighth, Green called for McGraw. One of the police dogs in the rightfield bullpen had gone for the reliever's glove when he reached for it to warm up.

"I think," said McGraw, "he was in love."

It had to end this way. McGraw's thigh-slapping, heart-patting finishes had characterized the Phillies' postseason run. All his life, the wild-eyed reliever had been pointing to this destination.

On the mound with a World Series to win.

"Nerve-wracking is the reason you play sports," he said. "You want to have your nerves wracked. If sports didn't wrack your nerves, you'd find something else to do."

He had been with two Mets' World Series teams. A nonfactor when they won in 1969, he had pitched a lot in the 1973 Series. But New York lost it to Oakland.

The Phillies had picked up McGraw, then age 30, before the 1975 season. They gave up John Stearns, Mac Scarce, and, ironically Del Unser to get him.

"I was pissed off," said Green, then the minor-league director. "Pope and Hughie had to fight like hell to sell me on that one. I didn't want to see them part with John Stearns, who was our top catching prospect."

McGraw's wackiness might have been hard to take on a losing club ("He's Irish and left-handed," said onetime Phillies owner Bill Giles, "an irrepressible combination."), but that's just when the Phillies started to win.

The 1979 season had been a nightmare. Ozark, he believed, never knew how to get the most out of him. He hurt his elbow early in this World Series season, but when he returned in mid-July, he was almost perfect.

The ball did what he demanded. He'd lie awake at night, imagining wonderful screwballs snapping past hitters. The next day, that's just what they did. The perfection stretched into the postseason. Then his arm grew heavy, his stuff turned average, and he felt like an overused 35-year-old pitcher. But the outs continued.

He needed just six more now.

The Tylenol wasn't helping McGraw much on this night. Adrenaline would have to carry him. He escaped the eighth inning having allowed only one run—when Wathan scored on Washington's sacrifice fly.

In the bottom of the eighth, the Phillies acted as if they didn't want to stand in the way of the destiny that was rolling noisily toward them.

Maddox, Trillo, and Bowa went down quickly.

◆ ◆ ◆

Everyone in the stands was on their feet when the ninth inning began.

"At last," these fans seemed to be thinking, "we get to see what this feels like."

Policemen stood in the dugouts and bullpens. The horsemen emerged from an outfield tunnel and rimmed the field. The dog units took their places—in the stands, along the dugouts, in front of the low railings that separated the seating area from the field.

At the sight of the horses striding across the outfield warning track, players and spectators looked as stunned as the tens of millions of viewers around the country who, with cable still in its infancy, made this the highest-rated World Series ever.

Had Frank Rizzo staged a coup?

McGraw fanned Otis but walked Aikens. Wathan and Onix Concepcion singled. At last, the Phillies reliever was out of gas.

"My arm was gone," he said. "It was numb, and I couldn't hardly feel the ball in my hand. I was very close to calling Dallas Green and having him come and get me."

The sensation in the Philadelphia crowd now grew more familiar, changing from joy to angst as the Royals rallied.

The year before, he had allowed four grand slams and earned the nickname "Grand Slam McGraw." If he gave one up now, Kansas City would be ahead and Danny Ozark and 1964 would have some undistinguished company in Phillies history.

"I was just hoping not to overthrow, trying to throw it down the middle and let my defense get involved," he said. "But I was very tired."

As White came to bat, McGraw took in the chaotic atmosphere. This was great, but he hoped it would all be over soon.

The Royals second baseman did him a favor, swinging at the first pitch and popping it up down the first-base line.

Boone and Rose converged as the stadium fell silent. The ball kicked out of the catcher's mitt. The crowd gasped. As Boone instinctively stuck out his bare hand, Rose's glove snatched the ball before it hit the turf.

"Before I even had time to react," said Boone, "Pete grabbed it."

With one swift motion, Rose had fulfilled his Phillies destiny.

"Just two aggressive guys trying to make a play," Rose explained.

The roar and the building anticipation rose even higher.

McGraw took another look around, seeking reassurance, motivation, some kind of sign. He saw the dogs, the K-9 Corps.

"Wait a minute," he thought. "'K' means strikeout, and this is the ninth inning. 'K-9'. There's my sign!"

It helped that Wilson, suddenly "Willie the K," was up. The Royals leadoff hitter already had struck out 11 times in the Series. Two had come in this game, and after each, Wilson looked completely baffled, tossing his bat down, gazing into the black sky for answers. The Phillies had him so confused he probably never saw the horses and dogs as he walked into the batter's box and drew a long breath.

McGraw's elbow was throbbing now. He didn't want to throw a screwball, but Boone convinced him he had to.

"Throw him one, just to put it in his head, and then we'll get him with fastballs," said Boone.

Wilson took a fastball for strike one. Then came the screwball. He fouled it off his foot. A fastball just missed high, and a huge roar died in the fans' throats.

Now McGraw exhaled. Boone called for a fastball away. McGraw delivered.

Wilson swung.

He missed.

The clock in left field, the one that rocked and twinkled in the explosion of noise, read 11:29 P.M.

The reliever opened his mouth wide and, arms outstretched, jumped into the air. All around him fans did the same. This, thought McGraw, is every baseball player's dream.

"I remember asking myself before I threw the ball, 'If this is supposed to be fun, why do I feel like I'm falling apart?'" McGraw said. "It took everything I had in me to keep myself from going nuts. But then I thought, 'You know, that's the fans' job, to go nuts. I'd better get back to business here. Standing out on the mound with the bases loaded and two outs and Willie Wilson up and 70,000 people watching in the arena and who knows how many watching on TV, that's what you dream about. Everytime you threw a pitch as a kid you thought about striking out Willie Mays to win a World Series. Then out of all the kids that were born from 1883, when the Phillies first started, and who loved baseball, I got to be the guy to throw that final pitch."

The impossible had happened. Not an impossible dream. Anything can happen in a dream. The impossible part had been imagining it could *really* occur.

Schmidt raced to the mound and, as promised, hurled himself onto McGraw. The pile expanded rapidly. Bowa bounced endlessly around it. A kid at the Christmas tree. Clusters of celebration erupted everywhere on the field, in the stands.

McGraw looked at his teammates and then up to the highest part of the enormous stadium, the 700 level.

"You take Keith Moreland, Kevin Saucier, Lonnie Smith, Marty Bystrom—they were rookies, and all of a sudden they were world champions," McGraw recalled thinking. "They hadn't been here six months. But that guy sitting up in the 700 level in centerfield who started going to games with his great-grandfather and grandfather and father and all those years of frustration and then all of a sudden the Phillies win a world championship. I think it meant more to him."

Minutes later, back in a Phillies clubhouse that had never accommodated so many smiles, NBC's Bryant Gumbel interviewed Green, Owens, and Carpenter.

The general manager couldn't speak. The 56-year-old man, who six weeks earlier had challenged his players to fight, bawled like a baby. He kissed Green, Carpenter, McGraw, and others and told them he loved them.

All over Philadelphia, fans were doing the same.

The City of Brotherly Love at last.

Chapter 10

 # A March into History

Once a century, even in Philadelphia, things ought to be allowed to turn out right.

JAYSON STARK, *PHILADELPHIA INQUIRER*

From the moment McGraw leaped into the air and the celebration ignited, a single refrain echoed around the city and its surrounding suburbs, nine words that indicated just how much pessimism a century of losing could sow:

"I never thought I'd live to see this day!"

But now that day was here. And no one had the slightest doubt as to how it ought to be lived.

According to police, in the dark, dizzying minutes before midnight, crowds of 5,000 or more assembled in at least 25 different locations across the area. Philadelphia was the "City of Neighborhoods" and every one of them partied.

In 1974, the Philadelphia Flyers' first Stanley Cup had triggered a wild outburst that was more riot than revelry. Area police, as the nationally televised display of dogs and horses during Game 6 demonstrated, had a game plan this time. They were going to use preemptive shows of force wherever possible.

Police moved in early at several locations. Much of their

attention focused on the intersection of Kensington and Allegheny avenues in working-class Kensington. Two thousand fans, many of them inebriated, had gathered there after the Phillies' division-clinching game in Montreal on October 4. More had come when the Phillies hung on to beat the Astros in the NLCS. "K & A," as residents called the intersection, was where their fathers had congregated after the Whiz Kids won in Brooklyn in 1950 and where their grandfathers probably had done the same in 1915. It was as if, by going there to celebrate, they were responding to some unseen force, something primal and perhaps even genetic.

These were people for whom sitting on the front steps on a sweltering summer night, drinking a cold Schmidt's, and listening to By Saam broadcast a Phillies game was a sacred tradition. Their immediate ancestors had passed down traditions like these along with their love of baseball. It helped explain how working-class people outlived the Great Depression. Most of their fathers and grandfathers had worked in the massive factories—Stetson Hats, Philco, Baldwin Locomotive—that made the neighborhood bustle through the first half of the century. Connie Mack Stadium wasn't too far away and on nice summer evenings, Kensington residents walked west on Lehigh Avenue to the old ballpark.

Now those factories were empty brick shells. And every week, it seemed, new "For Sale" signs sprouted up like weeds on these tiny blocks as the neighborhood's ethnic makeup shifted from Irish and Polish to African-American and Puerto Rican. The site where Connie Mack Stadium once stood was a litter-strewn vacant lot. The new stadium was way out on the southern edge of the city, its huge parking lots crowded with cars from the suburbs. From Kensington, you had to take two subways to get there.

But while baseball had abandoned them, somehow they remained fans. One of the few things that hadn't changed for these people, one of the few things that stamped them as real Philadelphians, was their passion for the Phillies.

At 10:30 P.M. with the Phillies ahead and Game 6 heading for its final innings, there was an eerie calm at the typically busy corner. Then, just about the time the ninth inning was starting, someone stuck his head out the front door of one of those narrow row homes and, according to police reports, yelled, "Come on. Let's do it!"

At the unseen clarion's call, bars and houses began to empty. The streets filled rapidly. Several thousand mingled there as they awaited a final score. By game's end, their numbers had doubled. One fan climbed atop the "Kensington" portion of the El-stop sign, high above the street. Holding on with one hand, he repeatedly drummed the sign's "Allegheny" half with the other. Others joined him. One girder acrobat lost his grip, but was caught by bystanders. Swinging there with them was an effigy of George Brett. A thick noose wound tightly around the dummy's neck. It was on fire.

Downtown, the bars were packed, too. In Taras Tavern on Green Street, owner and bartender Mo Taras served drinks as fast as he could pour them. Patrons, their eyes focused on the bar's television set, pushed him their money and gulped down their beer and liquor without ever looking down. When, after the game, a newspaper reporter asked Taras how he felt, he dabbed at his eyes and responded in throaty Italian.

"*Sono tanto felice che non poso parlare,*" he said. Someone translated for the reporter. "I am so happy, I cannot talk."

All throughout the city reports of tearful celebrants were as common as those of wildly ecstatic or drunken ones. The Phillies' triumph had awakened the ghosts. Everyone, it

seemed, had a bittersweet memory of a deceased friend or rela-
tive who had suffered with the Phillies and died unrewarded.
Fans mentioned over and over that, as happy as they were, their
one regret was that their father or brother or aunt couldn't be
there to savor it with them. One policeman at City Hall
remarked that he was so emotionally and physically elated that
it felt like someone had ripped open his chest and grabbed his
heart.

In suburban Delaware County, Phillies fan Bill Donaldson
wanted to share his postgame joy. His wife and boys were
asleep. Adrenaline pumping, he climbed the stairs to his bedroom. Opening the door, waiting for the light to wake his sleep-
ing wife, he saw her head lift slowly off the pillow. He held up
two fingers in a victory sign, wordlessly indicating to her that
his Phillies had won. Then, with a smile on his face, he walked
back downstairs, sat in his chair, and died of a massive heart
attack.

His young son Michael awoke sometime later to the rotat-
ing glare of a red light flashing outside his bedroom. It was only
the next morning, when he climbed into bed with his mother
and older brother, that he learned the light had come not from a
Phillies celebration but from the ambulance that carried his
dead father away.

"Everywhere you go in this city you hear stories like that
about that night," said McGraw. "People talk about the Phillies
winning the World Series like it was some spiritual event. Well,
it was a physical one, too. It grabbed fans, grabbed them deep
inside."

That morning after, October 22, 1980, the Vatican an-
nounced that it had decided to review its case against Galileo,
excommunicated as a heretic in 1633. Apparently, now that the
Phillies had won a World Series, it was no longer so hard to

believe, as the Italian scientist did, that the earth revolved around the sun.

◆ ◆ ◆

The winners' clubhouse produced a surreal atmosphere. Carlton celebrated behind closed doors. Some Phillies, well into the champagne by the time the clubhouse doors opened to the media, chanted obscenities at writers. Green invited President Carter, who had telephoned his congratulations, to abandon softball and come to Philadelphia to learn baseball. Owens wept continuously and, in a most un-baseball-like gesture, kissed whichever coach or player he could collar.

Once he retreated to his office and the media crowd dwindled to just a few local writers, Green grew reflective. He hinted that maybe he wouldn't return next season, that this one had been too trying. He tried to sum up this extraordinarily tumultuous season.

"No matter how talented you are, I think you've got to work every day to prepare yourself for the game and prepare yourself physically," he said. "We challenged them every single day. We wouldn't let them slip. If my coaching staff saw something wrong, they jumped. And if they didn't jump far enough, I jumped. We kept the pressure on the players from the time spring training started.

"The game plan was pretty simple. We wanted them to play every single day with their heart and soul, to recognize that this may be their last hurrah. Their way had not worked before. We had a game plan we thought could work, and we were going to keep reminding them that that's the way we were going to play. We felt if we could bring them together and make them recognize that they could play every day up to their talents, we could compete with anybody. It got to be a tough sell. We had a lot of adversity on that team that really went past just being clubhouse banter. There were some very difficult times, and the guys responded very well. Even though the message was screamed loud and clear, the guys had a tough time figuring it out until September."

◆ ◆ ◆

Down in Vero Beach, Florida, Green's forgotten predecessor watched the game on TV with his wife.

"We both had a couple of tears in our eyes," said Danny Ozark. "I wish I'd have been there to be a part of it. Maddox, Schmidt, Bowa, Boone, Luzinski, Bake, Ruthven, Carlton, Christenson, Reed, McGraw, those players all were with me. We developed the club together. We suffered together."

◆ ◆ ◆

By the time most of the Phillies had vacated Vet Stadium, navigated through the packs of revelers that lingered around the stadium, and got home, it was 4 A.M. Some of them never made it that far. Several players stayed at the Vet, and one group continued their party at Luzinski's South Jersey home.

Rising early the next day, giddy and hung over, they really weren't sure what to expect from the victory parade that the city had planned for 11:30 A.M. "I expected a few thousand people," said McBride. "No big thing." Some veterans like Bowa, Schmidt, Luzinski, and Boone recalled the raucous Flyers' celebration. As they dressed on a perfect autumn morning, they wondered if that was the kind of chaos that was in store for them.

Told they had to meet at the stadium at 10:30 A.M., several Phillies had to be talked into attending. While many of them lived year-round in the area, others were eager to get home.

They were weary. It had been an unusually long season. First there was all the talk of a strike. The nonstop bickering and newspaper headlines wore them down emotionally. And, finally, the delicious pressure that made the last month tingle drained them even more. For them, the 1980 baseball season felt like it had begun in the Eisenhower administration.

"It was the sweetest feeling in the world," said Schmidt. "But we were played out. Once the Series ended, a lot of us felt like, 'How did I possibly make it that far?' We were shot."

But, in the end, all of them except Reed showed up. They parked at the stadium and bused up to 18th Street and JFK Boulevard where the 11 flatbed trucks awaited them. At 11:17 A.M., Carlton, dressed incongruously in a three-piece suit, stepped off the bus there. The noise of those assembled knocked him backward. And when he looked up, his jaw nearly dropped to his loafers. The surrounding rooftops were jammed with screaming fans. It reminded some Phillies of the scene that greeted the Beatles' arrival in New York in 1964, when the airport terminal's roof appeared to sag beneath the weight of all those bouncing, screaming teenaged girls. Now, just a block away, Philadelphia's Greyhound bus terminal looked the same, like it might tip over from the crowds that lined the edges of its roof.

The city's liquor stores—operated by the state—were closed until 3 P.M., but many in the crowd carried sixpacks of beer they had purchased in bars or delicatessens. Schools were open but half empty. Upper Darby High, a school of 2,500 students just west of the city, reported 1,000 absences. The entrances to downtown offices bore signs that read, "Closed for Phillies parade." Banks, fearful that all the police would be tied up with the parade, shut their doors for its duration.

Police officials remarked that they had never seen anything

like this in Philadelphia. Crowd estimates varied from 750,000 to three million. One police captain said the throng clogging the two-mile route from City Hall to JFK Stadium was three times larger than the Flyers' victory parade—and nearly a million had assembled for that event.

The Phillies, their families, the team's front-office staff, bands, the media, and local and state politicians would make the journey on the big trucks. At first, the players, who occupied two of the flatbeds, felt odd and somewhat vulnerable standing atop them. "The people running the parade told us we were up high on the trucks so the people could all see us," recalled Owens. "But as it turned out, the best part of being up there was that we could see all the people. We were so much higher than them that it felt like we were in heaven."

Soon the Overbrook High band, bunched atop the first flatbed, broke into a marching tune. As the trucks started rolling, a spectator wearing a multi-colored fright wig and riding a bicycle darted out front and acted as an unofficial drum major, leading them down Market Street. Reaching City Hall, the parade turned right, left, and right again to reach Broad. That's when the Phillies' hearts stopped.

"Boy, my wife and I were tired," said Owens, "but when we saw all those people at the start of the parade, it just lifted you right up. We couldn't believe the crowds on Market Street. Then we turned onto Broad Street. I turned to her and said, 'Oh, my God!'"

It looked to them all as if some great red sea had been parted. Hundreds of thousands of fans, 20 and 30 deep in some spots, had reduced the wide thoroughfare into a narrow lane that stretched south as far as their eyes could see. Thousands more filled the roofs, balconies, and windows of the flanking buildings. They hung like Christmas angels from the horizontal traffic-light standards over Broad Street. They balanced them-selves on stop signs and narrow ledges. Some carried children on their shoulders. Almost everyone wore red. And all of them smiled—even those whose eyes were moist at the thought of this historic redemption.

"That was the thing I'll never forget," said Owens. "The smiles. You didn't see one person—not one—who wasn't smil-ing. And they were genuine smiles. We felt like we removed a cloud that had been hanging over the city's heads."

Construction workers waved from the girders of unfinished buildings. A distinguished-looking gentleman in a conservative gray suit applauded on the steps of the properly aristocratic Union League headquarters, exactly where Philadelphia's earli-est Republicans had stood to watch Abraham Lincoln's funeral cortege pass 115 years earlier. And from either side of the street, shredded paper and ticker tape fell like snow from the sun-filled skies.

"It was the most awesome sight I'd ever seen," said Bowa. "You knew then how long these people had been waiting for this, how much they cared about the Phillies."

A century's worth of stored-up good will spilled out onto Broad Street. As the parade rolled on, the Phillies grew more awestruck. Schmidt, Bowa, Boone, and Rose resembled those big-headed dolls that bobbed along on the dashboards of cars. One moment, their heads swiveled up in openmouthed wonder to observe and acknowledge the spectators situated high above. Then they would quickly lower them to wave and shout at those lining the street.

"It was such an incredible emotional high," said Schmidt. "You couldn't wipe the smile off your face, and neither could they."

Owens kept grabbing Green's hand and lifting it over their

heads the way a boxing referee signals a fight's winner. Players, even the coolest among them, made huge sweeping gestures with their arms to communicate with the noisy thousands. Schmidt, wearing a red sweater and sunglasses, at first tried to maintain his laid-back demeanor, trying, in *Daily News* columnist Stan Hochman's words, "to look cool, hoping he could fool his adrenal glands." The facade quickly fell away.

Fans tossed roses at them. They threw mementos of their allegiance—old pennants, worn caps, scorecards.

"I couldn't believe my eyes," said McBride. "There were millions of them crying, reaching out to shake our hands, give us flowers or cans of beer."

At Methodist and St. Agnes hospitals, nurses wheeled patients out onto the sidewalks or up onto the roofs. Green spotted some of the Methodist Hospital doctors who had so often operated on his players. He saluted them.

◆ ◆ ◆

The Phillies relaxed as the trucks moved past Veterans Stadium and the Spectrum and turned into JFK Stadium, the seldom-used 54-year-old facility that once hosted the best of the Army–Navy games and a Dempsey–Tunney fight. They descended from the moving platforms, were surrounded by security personnel, and were ushered into the horseshoe stadium. When they moved from the tunnel into the sunlight, more than 90,000 people, many of them having waited there all morning, erupted. The roar expanded as each player emerged. A few of them, Dickie Noles, Warren Brusstar, and others, had been drinking beer during the parade. They made an immediate U-turn to find a rest room. Their teammates stood on a makeshift platform and surveyed the remarkable scene. A few of them, overcome by the emotional spectacle of the last hour, had no defenses left. "We bawled like babies," said Elia.

"All the way down Broad Street, you kept thinking, 'Man, it can't get any better than this,' said John Vukovich. "And then we went into the stadium, and you heard all this noise and saw all those people. It just took your breath away."

This being Philadelphia, Mayor William Green and Pennsylvania Governor Richard Thornburgh were booed when they were introduced. Both politicians wisely made brief addresses. Then Phillies broadcaster Harry Kalas took the microphone to introduce the Phillies.

Bowa, who 23 days earlier had called these same fans "front-runners" and baseball's worst, now praised them, even if a smattering of boos could be detected. "This probably is the greatest moment in my entire life," said Bowa, wearing a cowboy hat. "I'm glad I can share it with the greatest fans in baseball."

Schmidt, who despite his penchant for foot-in-mouth comments to reporters usually said the appropriate thing in public, urged the spectators to "savor this championship."

An emotional Green gushed in words that suggested his speech had been lifted from a first-grade reader. "You people are beautiful," he said. "This team is beautiful. Everyone is beautiful."

Then finally, and appropriately, McGraw, holding up a *Philadelphia Daily News* with a front-page headline that blared "WE WIN!," finished up for one last time in 1980. His words cut right to the spirit of the moment. This world championship—and certainly this parade—was about more than baseball. It was about a city shaking free of a complex.

"Throughout baseball history," he yelled, "Philadelphia has taken a back seat to New York City. Well, New York City, you can take this world championship and stick it."

It was all over so fast, like one of those holiday feasts that takes forever to prepare and, though savored and long recalled, vanishes in an instant. As fans departed Center City and JFK Stadium that afternoon, they had been sated. It would take at least another century to work up that kind of appetite again. If the overriding question for players and fans the previous night had been, "What will it feel like?" less than 24 hours later it had become, "How can we possibly top this?"

The 1981 season began with a carryover effect. Mike Schmidt, 1980 regular-season and World Series MVP awards on his mantle, began to play like a man who was sure he was headed for Cooperstown. "Let's just say confidence and relaxation were never a problem for me after 1980," he said. The Phillies were brilliant early. They were 34–21 and in first place when the strike they had fortuitously avoided in 1980 hit at last.

Somehow, in the baseball-less weeks that preceded the resumption of what would be a split season, an era ended, a spirit succumbed. The Phillies were diminished. They went 25–27, drove Green to another obscenity-laden tirade with their inconsistency, and were eliminated by second-half NL East champ Montreal in a divisional play-off series necessitated by the strike.

Luzinski, as he long had feared, was gone before the season started, traded to the Chicago White Sox. Then, after the 1981 season, Bowa went there, too, to the Cubs, in a terrible deal that saw the Phillies throw in future Hall of Famer Ryne Sandberg for Ivan DeJesus. That 1981 season was the last for Boone and McBride in Philadelphia, and Trillo stayed only another year.

Green, who even in the midst of the post–World Series celebration had questioned whether he wanted to return, also was lured away after 1981 as the Cubs granted him control of their baseball operations. His decision was made easier when, in a stunning off-season development, Ruly Carpenter decided to sell the ballclub his grandfather had purchased.

Dismayed by soaring salaries in general and Claudell Washington's in particular, Carpenter sold the team to a consortium headed by Bill Giles, the vice president in charge of promotions and broadcasting, for $30 million. Giles was on the long list of people Green couldn't get along with, and the manager jumped at the Cubs' offer. The transition marked the beginning of a decline in Owens's influence, too, though the GM would again return to the dugout midway through the 1983 season after Pat Corrales was fired despite managing a first-place team.

With Schmidt, Carlton, and aging imports like Tony Perez and Joe Morgan, the 1983 Phillies—the Wheeze Kids—won another pennant. But it was an illusion, a last gasp. Baltimore beat them four straight times in a five-game World Series, and another decade of all-too-familiar Phillies futility ensued.

McGraw retired in 1984. Before that season, Rose, who had been benched during the 1983 World Series and eventually released, had returned to Cincinnati. He broke Ty Cobb's hit record there and became the Reds manager. But soon his career was over and his reputation forever stained by a gambling scandal that made him a baseball outcast.

Many of the 1980 Phillies fringe players—Unser, Brusstar, Saucier, Lerch, Christenson—faded away much more quietly, without ever making another big splash, their small but significant roles in a historic moment complete. Lonnie Smith became a fixture in World Series contests for a number of teams over the next decade and a half, but battled drug problems along the way. Noles's abilities were overwhelmed by booze, and he became one of the first big-league players placed on the disabled list because of alcoholism.

"If you're not careful," said Unser, who has held a number

of jobs in the Phillies front office, a few years later, "you can fall into the trap where you think everything in life after the World Series is anticlimax. The truth is our lives are just beginning. I've got it worked out now, but for a while, I was depressed."

◆　◆　◆

Nineteen eighty was a crossroads year for the Phillies and baseball. It was the end of the Carpenter era, the end of the Schmidt-Luzinski-Carlton-Boone-Bowa nucleus that had played together for eight seasons, the beginning of a rapid decline in the farm system Owens and Green had built. Veterans Stadium, a showcase in its first decade, quickly became an anachronism with its antiseptic atmosphere and artificial surface. Cable television was transforming fans' viewership patterns, and the enormous ratings and shares that the 1980 World Series attracted—Game 6 drew the largest audience in World Series history—would not again be matched. More TV outlets meant more televised sport, and baseball's fan base splintered like dry wood.

Free agency, still something of an oddity then, was about to radically transform baseball. Fourteen of the 1980 Phillies had come up through the system. By the time the 1993 Phillies won a pennant, only two regulars and none of their rotation were Philadelphia-bred.

"Free agency has done many, many good things for the sport," said Schmidt. "But, for sure, there is not the town loyalty nowadays that there was, and that might have ended in 1980. We were one of the last teams that was homegrown."

◆　◆　◆

In October of 2000, the Phillies were comfortably adrift again in their familiar orbit. The bottom of the standings. A typical Philadelphia street fight over the location of a new ballpark had left them in antiquated Veterans Stadium long after other clubs had inhabited a new generation of retro stadiums. On TV broadcasts of their games, cameras focused tightly on the players so that the vast blue sea of empty seats got minimal exposure.

Their shrinking fan base was aging rapidly, and while those people tended to recall 1980 with a misty-eyed fondness—in a *Daily News* end-of-millennium poll, it was picked as Philadelphia's greatest sports moment—a new generation raised on the immediacy of ESPN could hardly care less.

The Phillies finished the 2000 season with their 14th losing record in 15 years. Manager Terry Francona was fired. Club officials pondered their options about a replacement. Whatever they did, it was essential that they shore up their fan base. They decided they needed to summon up some good feeling, to sell some seats, to stir things up. They needed a hero.

So they hired Larry Bowa.

They hired Bowa despite his disastrous, expletive-filled, and brief tenure as San Diego's manager a decade earlier. They hired him despite all his bad feelings for Bill Giles, his comments about the local fans, his temper. They hired him despite concerns that it was entirely possible he might one day drive a player to murder.

They hired him for one reason—1980.

"That was one hell of a year," said Green, by then back with the Phillies as a senior executive, on the connection. "I'm sure the people here remember 1980, and they remember the part Bo played in that season. It's been 20 years now, but it's not ever going to be forgotten."

Earlier that year, on June 17, the Phillies marked the 20th anniversary of their lone world championship team. Only three of the team members did not attend the event, which could not fill the Vet. Espinosa was long dead. Bowa, then a Seattle Mariners third-base coach and miffed at Giles over some decades-old slight, refused to come. And Rose, still unrepentant, was not permitted to be part of the ceremonies because his ban prohibited him from attending any official major-league function.

A night earlier, in an effort to recapture something from the greatest moment in their history, the victory parade, the old Phillies rode a short distance down Broad Street in convertibles.

Only about 250 spectators watched.

"I can't believe it's been 20 years since these guys won," said George Hollingsworth, 56, of South Philadelphia, "and we're still waiting for another."

Bibliography

Books

Anderson, Dave. *Pennant Races,* Doubleday, New York, 1994.

Bodley, Hal. *The Team That Wouldn't Die*, Serendipity Press, Wilmington, Delaware, 1981.

Dolson, Frank. *The Philadelphia Story*, Icarus Press, South Bend, Indiana, 1981.

Hageman, William and Warren Wilbert. *New York Yankees: Seasons of Glory*, Jonathan David Publishers, New York, 1999.

Helyar, John. *Lords of the Realm*, Villard Books, New York, 1994.

Honig, Donald. *The Philadelphia Phillies: An Illustrated History*, Simon & Schuster, New York, 1982.

Kashatus, Bill. *Connie Mack's '29 Triumph*, McFarland and Co., Jefferson, North Carolina, 1999.

Kuklick, Bruce. *To Every Thing a Season*, Princeton University Press, Princeton, New Jersey, 1991.

Lewis, Allen. *The Philadelphia Phillies: A Pictorial History*, JCP Corp. of Virginia, Virginia Beach, Virginia, 1981.

McCarver, Tim, with Ray Robinson. *Oh, Baby, I Love It*, Villard Books, New York, 1987.

Okrent, Daniel and Steve Wulf. *Baseball Anecdotes*, Harper & Row, New York, 1990.

Orodenker, Richard. *The Phillies Reader*, Temple University Press, Philadelphia, 1996.

Peary, Danny. *We Played the Game*, Hyperion, New York, 1994.

Reichler, Joseph L. *The World Series: A 75th Anniversary*, Simon & Schuster, New York, 1978.

Roberts, Robin and C. Paul Rogers III. *The Whiz Kids and the 1950 Pennant*, Temple University Press, Philadelphia, 1996.

Thorn, John and Pete Palmer. *Total Baseball*, Fourth Edition, Viking, New York, 1995.

Periodicals

Newspapers

Philadelphia Bulletin
Philadelphia Daily News
Philadelphia Inquirer
New York Daily News

New York Post
New York Times
Kansas City Star
Washington Post

Magazines

Sports Illustrated
Newsweek
Time

Videos

Glory Days: The Story of the 1980 World Champion Phillies, The Philadelphia Phillies, 2000.

Index